THE WAY
PEOPLE
LIVE

Life in Castro's Cuba

Titles in The Way People Live series include:

Cowboys in the Old West
Games of Ancient Rome
Life Aboard the Space Shuttle
Life Aboard the Space Station
Life Among the Aztecs
Life Among the Great Plains Indians
Life Among the Ibo Women of Nigeria
Life Among the Inca
Life Among the Indian Fighters
Life Among the Pirates
Life Among the Puritans
Life Among the Samurai
Life Among the Vikings
Life During the American Revolution
Life During the Black Death
Life During the Crusades
Life During the Dust Bowl
Life During the French Revolution
Life During the Gold Rush
Life During the Great Depression
Life During the Middle Ages
Life During the Renaissance
Life During the Roaring Twenties
Life During the Russian Revolution
Life During the Spanish Inquisition
Life in a Japanese American Internment
    Camp
Life in America During the 1960s
Life in a Medieval Castle
Life in a Medieval Monastery
Life in a Medieval Village
Life in an Amish Community
Life in a Nazi Concentration Camp
Life in Ancient Athens
Life in Ancient China
Life in Ancient Egypt
Life in Ancient Greece
Life in Ancient Rome
Life in a Wild West Show

Life in Berlin
Life in Charles Dickens's England
Life in Communist Russia
Life in Genghis Khan's Mongolia
Life in Hong Kong
Life in Moscow
Life in the Amazon Rain Forest
Life in the American Colonies
Life in the Australian Outback
Life in the Elizabethan Theater
Life in the Hitler Youth
Life in the Negro Baseball League
Life in the North During the Civil War
Life in the South During the Civil War
Life in the Stone Age
Life in the Warsaw Ghetto
Life in Tokyo
Life in War-Torn Bosnia
Life of a Medieval Knight
Life of a Nazi Soldier
Life of a Roman Gladiator
Life of a Roman Slave
Life of a Roman Soldier
Life of a Slave on a Southern Plantation
Life on Alcatraz
Life on a Medieval Pilgrimage
Life on an African Slave Ship
Life on an Everest Expedition
Life on a New World Voyage
Life on an Indian Reservation
Life on Ellis Island
Life on the American Frontier
Life on the Oregon Trail
Life on the Pony Express
Life on the Underground Railroad
Life Under the Jim Crow Laws
Life Under the Taliban

THE WAY
PEOPLE
LIVE

Life in Castro's Cuba

by John M. Dunn

LUCENT
BOOKS®

THOMSON
—————✦—————™
GALE

San Diego • Detroit • New York • San Francisco • Cleveland • New Haven, Conn. • Waterville, Maine • London • Munich

LIBRARY OF CONGRESS CATALOGING-IN-PUBLICATION DATA

Dunn, John M.
Life in Castro's Cuba/ by John M. Dunn.
p. cm. — (The way people live)
Includes bibliographical references and index.
Contents: Living under the heel of Fidel Castro—Getting by in Castro's Cuba: no es facil
(it is not easy)—Getting along in Cuba: social structure and human relationships—
Literacy for all, Castro style—Trying to stay healthy—Seeking an escape in leisure time—
Buoying the Cuban spirit—Dissidence and departure.
ISBN 1-59018-464-5 (lib.: alk. paper)
I. Title. II. Series.

$22.96
9/05

Printed in the United States of America

Contents

FOREWORD
  Discovering the Humanity in Us All   6

INTRODUCTION
  Cuba: A Troubled Paradise   8

CHAPTER ONE
  Living Under the Heel of Fidel Castro   12

CHAPTER TWO
  Getting By in Castro's Cuba:
  No Es Fácil (It Is Not Easy)   22

CHAPTER THREE
  Getting Along in Cuba:
  Social Structure and Human Relationships   32

CHAPTER FOUR
  Literacy for All, Castro Style   44

CHAPTER FIVE
  Trying to Stay Healthy   54

CHAPTER SIX
  Seeking an Escape in Leisure Time   64

CHAPTER SEVEN
  Buoying the Cuban Spirit   76

CHAPTER EIGHT
  Dissidence and Departure   86

  Notes   96
  For Further Reading   100
  Works Consulted   101
  Index   105
  Picture Credits   111
  About the Author   112

Discovering the Humanity in Us All

Books in The Way People Live series focus on groups of people in a wide variety of circumstances, settings, and time periods. Some books focus on different cultural groups, others, on people in a particular historical time period, while others cover people involved in a specific event. Each book emphasizes the daily routines, personal and historical struggles, and achievements of people from all walks of life.

To really understand any culture, it is necessary to strip the mind of the common notions we hold about groups of people. These stereotypes are the archenemies of learning. It does not even matter whether the stereotypes are positive or negative; they are confining and tight. Removing them is a challenge that is not easily met, as anyone who has ever tried it will admit. Ideas that do not fit into the templates we create are unwelcome visitors—ones we would prefer remain quietly in a corner or forgotten room.

The cowboy of the Old West is a good example of such confining roles. The cowboy was courageous, yet soft-spoken. His time (it is always a he, in our template) was spent alternatively saving a rancher's daughter from certain death on a runaway stagecoach, or shooting it out with rustlers. At times, of course, he was likely to get a little crazy in town after a trail drive, but for the most part, he was the epitome of inner strength. It is disconcerting to find out that the cowboy is human, even a bit childish. Can it really be true that cowboys would line up to help the

cook on the trail drive grind coffee, just hoping he would give them a little stick of peppermint candy that came with the coffee shipment? The idea of tough cowboys vying with one another to help "Coosie" (as they called their cooks) for a bit of candy seems silly and out of place.

So is the vision of Eskimos playing video games and watching MTV, living in prefab housing in the Arctic. It just does not fit with what "Eskimo" means. We are far more comfortable with snow igloos and whale blubber, harpoons and kayaks.

Although the cultures dealt with in Lucent's The Way People Live series are often historically and socially well known, the emphasis is on the personal aspects of life. Groups of people, while unquestionably affected by their politics and their governmental structures, are more than those institutions. How do people in a particular time and place educate their children? What do they eat? And how do they build their houses? What kinds of work do they do? What kinds of games do they enjoy? The answers to these questions bring these cultures to life. People's lives are revealed in the particulars and only by knowing the particulars can we understand these cultures' will to survive and their moments of weakness and greatness.

This is not to say that understanding politics does not help to understand a culture. There is no question that the Warsaw ghetto, for example, was a culture that was brought about by the politics and social ideas of Adolf

Hitler and the Third Reich. But the Jews who were crowded together in the ghetto cannot be understood by the Reich's politics. Their life was a day-to-day battle for existence, and the creativity and methods they used to prolong their lives is a vital story of human perseverance that would be denied by focusing only on the institutions of Hitler's Germany. Knowing that children as young as five or six outwitted Nazi guards on a daily basis, that Jewish policemen helped the Germans control the ghetto, that children attended secret schools in the ghetto and even earned diplomas—these are the things that reveal the fabric of life, that can inspire, intrigue, and amaze.

Books in The Way People Live series allow both the casual reader and the student to see humans as victims, heroes, and onlookers. And although humans act in ways that can fill us with feelings of sorrow and revulsion, it is important to remember that "hero," "predator," and "victim" are dangerous terms. Heaping undue pity or praise on people reduces them to objects, and strips them of their humanity.

Seeing the Jews of Warsaw only as victims is to deny their humanity. Seeing them only as they appear in surviving photos, staring at the camera with infinite sadness, is limiting, both to them and to those who want to understand them. To an object of pity, the only appropriate response becomes "Those poor creatures!" and that reduces both the quality of their struggle and the depth of their despair. No one is served by such two-dimensional views of people and their cultures.

With this in mind, The Way People Live series strives to flesh out the traditional, two-dimensional views of people in various cultures and historical circumstances. Using a wide variety of primary quotations—the words not only of the politicians and government leaders, but of the real people whose lives are being examined—each book in the series attempts to show an honest and complete picture of a culture removed from our own by time or space.

By examining cultures in this way, the reader will notice not only the glaring differences from his or her own culture, but also will be struck by the similarities. For indeed, people share common needs—warmth, good company, stability, and affirmation from others. Ultimately, seeing how people really live, or have lived, can only enrich our understanding of ourselves.

Cuba: A Troubled Paradise

In 1959, when a radical, violent, brilliant, ruthless young lawyer named Fidel Castro led a successful armed revolt against Cuba's dictator, Fulgencio Batista, many Cubans hoped that decades of repression were at an end. Castro and his fellow revolutionaries promised social, economic, educational, and medical reforms, winning acclaim from both Cubans and foreign observers. Much of this public support, however, soon vanished when Castro imposed a new dictatorship that eventually proved to be more tyrannical and murderous than the regime he had helped destroy. Instead of a free and democratic Cuba, Castro chose to forge a Communist state based on the principles of German philosopher Karl Marx and the Russian revolutionary Vladimir Lenin, both of whom advocated total government control of society to meet the basic economic needs of all citizens.

Castro's forces quickly went to work restructuring Cuba. They imprisoned and executed many leaders and supporters of the Batista government. Castro banned all religious activity and ordered the arrest of anyone who criticized him. His troops confiscated all farms larger than one thousand acres and seized businesses and industries, including many that were American owned, and placed them under government control. The U.S. government retaliated by cutting off all shipments of goods to Cuba, except for food and medicine.

Castro soon proved to be more than a disciple of modern communism. He was also a megalomaniac who dreamed of dominating Latin America under a Communist banner and waging a war against the United States— a country whose government Castro came to despise and consider an enemy of Cuba.

Following Castro's rise to power, police arrested thousands of Cubans. Many were dissenters who wanted democratic reforms and who were outraged by Castro's actions. Others had no idea why they had been arrested. Most of those arrested were locked up in prisons where they lived for years in squalid conditions and were beaten and tortured. Critics of Castro's regime claim that thousands of people were executed by firing squads.

Alarmed by Castro's brutality and tyranny, a flood of Cubans left the island to live in the United States and other countries. Many of them were Cuba's educated professionals— engineers, doctors, nurses, teachers, and businesspeople. Without their help, Castro faced a daunting challenge of rebuilding Cuban society.

Some of these exiles resettled in Guatemala, where they created a militia trained for an invasion of Cuba to drive Castro from power. In April 1961, with limited U.S. backing, they fought Castro's forces at a place known as the Bay of Pigs and met a crushing defeat. Though Castro gloated over his victory, he also feared another attack, one that would have stronger backing from the United States. For help he turned to the Soviet Union, then the world's leading Communist power and the biggest geopolitical rival of the United States.

Castro further tightened his grip on Cuban society. He controlled Cuba's newspapers and broadcast companies. The only legal political party was the Communist Party. Castro combined the power of the nation's military and police to create a huge force to spy on his fellow citizens. His agents used fear, intimidation, and violence to force millions of Cubans to bend to his personal will.

Those who admire Castro insist that he desired not just personal power but was, and still is, also motivated by a strong desire to improve the lives of the people, especially the working poor. Castro rejected capitalism, however, as a means of bringing about these

Since 1959 Fidel Castro (center) has led a Communist regime that exercises total control over all aspects of Cuban society.

improvements. In his view capitalism is corrupt and unjust and inevitably causes inequality among people. Instead Castro imposed state control of Cuba's society in order to ensure equality. Poor Cubans cheered as Castro reduced rents, lowered telephone rates, and established land reform. He also launched a literacy campaign and set up socialized medicine to provide all Cubans with at least basic access to education and health care.

Not content to simply consolidate his revolution's gains at home, Castro also built up Cuba's armed forces and sent them abroad to back various Communist insurgencies in Africa, Latin America, and the Caribbean. During the 1970s Cuban troops took part in bloody, armed conflicts in Zaire, Ethiopia, Angola, and Congo, among other places. In 1983 they also took part in fighting against U.S. troops in the island nation of Grenada. Castro also provided other forms of support to Communist movements in Puerto Rico, Venezuela, and Bolivia.

Castro's efforts to establish Cuba as a major world power met with little success, however. As the twentieth century drew to a close, even his dream of improving the everyday lives of most Cubans had faded. Cuba's gains in education and medicine were eventually reversed. Most of these reversals were attributable to the collapse of the Soviet Union in 1991. For decades, the Soviet Union had subsidized Cuba, buying Cuban sugar and providing commodities like fuel and food at bargain prices. But when the Soviet Union collapsed, its $6 billion in annual subsidies to the Cuban economy vanished. This loss, plus an ongoing American trade embargo and Castro's own incompetence as a leader, caused a severe economic depression in Cuba in the 1990s. In response to the challenges, Castro announced that Cuba had entered a Tiempo Especial (Special Time) and demanded that the Cuban people make personal sacrifices, as if they were at war. Cubans now had to get

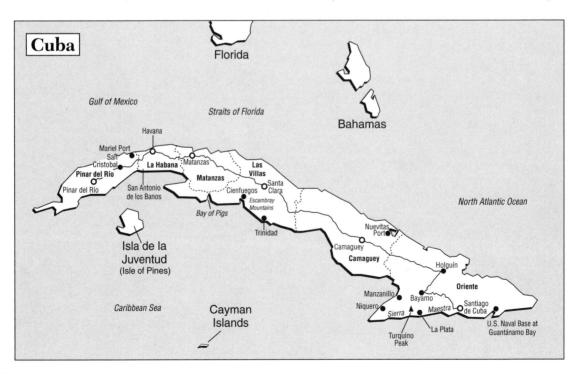

along with less food, clothing, fuel, medicine, and other staples. Many would have to forage or prostitute themselves to stay alive.

Though the worst of the Special Time may be over, life for most Cubans remains austere and hard. Deprived of liberty, oppressed and intimidated, millions live on the edge of poverty and have little hope that things will be dramatically better for them or their children. As a Cuban professor told American travel writer Christopher Hunt, "Cubans are like people watching a movie about their own lives. They know there's a bad ending. They just don't know which bad ending."[1]

Living Under the Heel of Fidel Castro

Fidel Castro controls the lives of 11.1 million people. In fact, daily life for all Cubans is inseparable from his decisions. For better and for worse, Castro has had a long time to make his mark on Cuban society. He is a totalitarian leader who has wielded power longer than any other dictator in the world. By 2003 he had matched wits with ten successive American presidents.

Castro has become indistinguishable from the Cuban power structure. He allows no political opposition. No law exists without his blessing. He is at the helm of the Cuban economy. More than anyone else he ultimately decides what kinds of jobs Cubans will have and how much they will be paid. This is possible because Cuba is a Socialist state, meaning that the government controls the work most Cubans do.

Cuba's dictator lays claim to many titles that testify to his vast personal power. He is commander in chief of the military, president, head of government, and the first secretary of the Communist Party. He also personally picks the members of the Politburo, the group that steers the Communist Party. The main purpose of Cuba's 601-member National Assembly of the People's Power is to approve policies and decisions made by Cuba's governing body—the Council of State, which Castro also controls.

Castro's policies determine which of his fellow citizens may visit other countries and who, if anyone, may speak freely to the outside world. Cuban censors monitor television shows, movies, musical performances, and art exhibitions. They censor authors and artists and ban those works they find offensive. Cuba's constitution gives these officials the authority to do this. Although Article 33 of the constitution promises freedom of expression, it also states that "editions of books, pamphlets, recordings, films, periodicals, or publications of whatever nature that attack the good reputation of persons, the social order, or the public peace, may be suppressed."[2]

The government even controls Cubans' leisure time activities. For example, state-controlled beaches, resorts, and hotels that serve as tourist destinations are off-limits to any Cubans who are not employed at these places. Cubans are even forbidden by their own government to merely meet with friends or relatives visiting from a foreign country and staying at one of the hotels. Nor can Cubans' eat at state-run tourist restaurants, which are stocked with an array of meats, fresh fruits, and vegetables unavailable to most Cubans. State officials worry that hungry Cubans would resent seeing the luxuries enjoyed by foreigners. The government also wants to prevent Cubans from meeting foreigners and receiving uncensored information about the outside world.

Cuba's dictator also exerts great sway over what students are taught in school and which students get into a university. Castro has the power to decide if and how religious groups can congregate to worship. He decides if Cubans go to war. In addition, he has the sole authority to set foreign policy. Cuba has neither a freely elected legislature nor an independent judicial system that can override his dictates. Even though the Cuban constitution states that "the organization of political parties and association is free,"[3] no political party except the Communist Party can run candidates for office. As Castro once told a reporter, Cuba does not need opposition parties because unity, rather than diversity of political thought, is of paramount importance. Castro's police arrest those who criticize him, his policies, or the government, and judges loyal to Castro impose harsh sentences against

The Views of a Castro Loyalist

In his book *Cuba—Going Back*, Cuban American Tony Mendoza recounts many of his encounters with the people of the land of his birth. Though most of the Cubans he interviewed expressed extreme dislike for Castro and his policies, others remained supportive. One of these Castro loyalists is Paquita, a professor at the University of Havana, whose exchange of views with Mendoza are recorded in this passage from the book.

"I [Mendoza] told them that as an artist I had always been disturbed by Fidel's famous statement, which he made at a meeting of writers and artists in 1961, where he laid out the guidelines for what would be permissible: 'With the Revolution, everything. Against the Revolution, nothing.' . . . Did the people at the university, especially those in the arts, see any kind of problem with Fidel's guidelines?

'No,' Paquita said . . . .

'Why not?'

'Because we are realists. The Revolution has a very powerful enemy ninety miles from our shore, and the enemy has many agents and sympathizers within our country. We can't allow our enemies to attack us with impunity. We have a right to defend ourselves. . . . We want this project to continue.'

'What project are you talking about?'

'Socialism. The Cuban Revolution. It's a beautiful project.'

'Still, if the project is that good, shouldn't it be able to withstand some criticism, some opposing positions? . . . '

'One can criticize here. We allow criticism. What we don't allow is counterrevolutionaries, people who intend to destroy the state. People say whatever they want, in the bus, in the street. I take the bus every day and I hear people complaining about everything, about the government. That's their right.'

'Yes, but can they complain about the government on television, or in the press?'

'Well, not there.'

'Why not?'

'We have a different system here. We believe in . . . [creating social unity], or nothing will get accomplished. We don't believe in the chaos of the multiparty system. . . . We welcome constructive criticism, but we don't want anyone to tear it down. That's not constructive. What we want to do is fix it up.'

I let that go and . . . [asked about the self-employed workers]. . . . I felt they were being abused by the government, whose long lists of excessive restrictions and fees seemed designed to drive them out of business. . . . Why was the government so afraid of the *paladar* owner succeeding?

'The answer is very simple. If the *paladar* owner doesn't have restrictions, he will become very rich. This is a socialist state. We do not permit inequalities. We do not have rich people here.'"

these critics. They have sentenced some of their fellow citizens to prison for up to twenty years and more for such offenses. Others have been executed. Government spies search neighborhoods and workplaces for fellow citizens who are deemed by Castro and his followers to be disloyal.

Castro's presence seems to be everywhere. Dressed in olive-green military fatigues, he appears at massive rallies. His graying, bearded image appears on television, and he is heard on the radio, haranguing the Cuban people for hours at a time. The official newspaper, *El Granma*—named after a boat Castro used during his successful revolution —records every word of his speeches. He is the official spokesman for the Cuban Communist Party. He purports to speak on behalf of the Cuban people, although he has never in forty-four years sought their consent in a free election in which candidates from opposition parties could participate. The state orchestrates parades and mass rallies in support of what Castro and the Communists do for the people. Many Cubans have little choice but to participate in these staged events, or face dire

Castro often delivers lengthy speeches at massive rallies, and every word is reprinted in the state-controlled newspaper.

consequences. In her book *Cuba Diaries: An American Housewife in Havana*, Isadora Tattlin reveals at least one way the Cuban government has to ensure mass participation: "A diplomat who was . . . [at a recent parade attended by half a million people] tells us it was impressive, how they mobilized marchers through their jobs; if you didn't go, you risked losing your job, or being demoted."[4]

Cubans commonly refer to their leader simply as "Fidel." Most use his first name, however, as a means of designation rather than as an expression of affection. Admirers call him El Commandante (Commander), Commandante en Jefe (Commander in Chief), or Nuestro Jefe (Our Chief). Many Cubans, however, are afraid even to mention his name. Ever fearful that a colleague, friend, or even a family member may turn them in to the police for showing disrespect to Castro, they pretend to stroke an invisible beard with their fingers to indicate when they are talking about their leader.

Spies Everywhere

People have good reason to be afraid because spies are everywhere, even in their own neighborhoods. The Cuban government provides for the basic needs of the Cuban people, supplying electricity, water, housing, health care, schools, and enough food to prevent starvation, but it demands absolute loyalty in return. State officials also have little use for those who complain about how the government is run and do not welcome constructive criticism. Castro, in fact, views most political opinions that vary from his own to be antirevolutionary and therefore illegal.

To ensure that Cubans remain loyal to Castro's regime, state security officers spy on everyone, especially writers, teachers, and community leaders. Government officials routinely wiretap the telephones of Cuban citizens and foreigners. Undercover agents and informers even keep watch on other government officials to make sure they do not stray from what the Communist Party expects them to say and do. The Committee for the Defense of the Revolution (CDR) is the government entity responsible for this domestic surveillance, and its agents seem to be everywhere. Whether they are at work or off-duty, Cubans are subject to scrutiny.

The CDR also recruits spies among ordinary Cubans to watch their neighbors for signs of antigovernment behavior. These spies are even expected to report the domestic problems of married couples. People of all ages serve as CDR spies. Cuban American Manuel Caberio recalls, "My mother was a member of her local CDR when she was just 13. At the time, she believed in Castro's rhetoric and was willing to stand guard duty in her neighborhood from 11:30 P.M. to 3:00 A.M. looking for any suspicious or anti-revolutionary activity."[5] Caberio's mother no longer spies on her neighbors. She now lives in the United States, an escapee from a society that expects youngsters to mistrust their neighbors.

Because of the constant presence of government spies, most Cubans are careful of what they say and do in public. Many have learned, to their lasting regret, that they must be cautious even at home among their loved ones, since Cubans are taught from childhood to report anyone—family members, friends, and coworkers—who disagrees with Castro.

Repressive Measures

Besides watching its citizens closely, like all other totalitarian governments, Castro's regime limits their exposure to ideas that come from

Cubans must be constantly on guard that they do not say or do anything that arouses the suspicions of the Communist dictatorship and makes them vulnerable to punishment. As writer and journalist Carlos Alberto Montaner points out in *Journey to the Heart of Cuba*, spies and informants are everywhere. Eight million are "cederistas," members of Castro's Committees for the Defense of the Revolution (CDR), a neighborhood watch network that keeps detailed records of Cubans' personel information and activities. This constant surveillance creates a climate of suspicion, distrust, and fear.

"Nobody knows for sure who, within the CDR, are direct informants. Yet every Cuban knows that the CDR spies on everyone, and is, in turn, spied upon. . . . Mutual distrust is one of the consistent elements of totalitarian societies, and the first thing families teach the children is to distrust and to pretend, for the child's chance of not running afoul of the repressive machinery will depend on his skill in those two behaviors. At the same time, that family training, the development of cynicism and lying as means of protection, helps convince the child that the system is invincible and that it would be futile to try to oppose it. There is no sense in fighting. Survival is achieved by faking it. There is no point in running risks by defending dangerous principles. Sacrificing oneself for others—in a community of informers—would be idiocy.

How is this repressive machinery structured? Every CDR regularly reports to a zone committee, which in turn reports to a municipal, then a provincial, and finally a national committee. From the zone committee, all the information is gathered by the professional police officers, who feed the insatiable computers of the Ministry of the Interior. No one can escape its magnifying glass. Everyone has a political dossier [file]. Even the most harmless citizen has an assigned officer in charge of monitoring his file, simply because you never know where an enemy of the fatherland may be hiding. And the term 'everyone' includes minors, for the cumulative [growing] dossier begins the moment when the child is registered in school."

outside the government and the country. It takes extreme precautions to limit meetings between Cuba's intellectuals and their professional colleagues in other countries. The state also discourages or punishes those who develop their own ideas and theories if these thoughts seem to contradict existing policies or threaten to embarass Castro. Government officials do not always arrest and jail those they suspect lack loyalty to the regime, but they do routinely withhold or take away visas and travel privileges or anything that is of value to the suspected dissidents. Castro's agents even use blackmail and violence to keep people in line.

Everyone Serves the State

Of all the ways the government has of keeping Cubans in line politically, one of the most effective is the threat that straying can cost one his or her job. This is possible because the government controls most of the employment in Cuba. It sets all salaries and wages for almost all jobs. It also demands that workers obtain state permission to change jobs. The government also maintains a cumulative labor record on all workers during their entire working lives. In addition to containing data such as daily attendance and job performance, these dossiers keep tabs on workers' ideological history. Any antigovernment word or deed witnessed by supervisors is written down. Workers whose cumulative records designate them as antirevolutionary may find that they are banned from most, if not all, forms of employment for years, perhaps even for life.

Responding to Castro's Dictatorial Control

Cubans react in various ways to Castro and his dictatorship. Some adore him, but many more hate him. Almost all fear him. His critics argue that he is a murderous tyrant who has destroyed basic human liberties, stifled dreams and aspirations, and turned Cuba into an island prison, not a tropical paradise. Some Cubans would love to kill him; others eagerly await the day he dies and his hold over Cuba vanishes.

Others, however, idolize Castro, though their numbers may be dwindling. For many Cubans, Castro is a revolutionary hero who removed an unpopular dictator and who has defiantly stood up to the United States. Such die-hard supporters praise the Cuban

The Cuban government tightly controls the country's job market. Here, a group of sugar-mill workers tends to a vegetable patch after the government closed their mill.

A mural glorifies the efforts of the Committee for the Defense of the Revolution (CDR). In reality, the CDR exposes political dissidents.

revolution and believe Castro has done his country a great service by raising living standards and providing basic services for the Cuban people. "We are proud of our revolution," one Castro supporter told travel writer Christopher Baker. "North Americans don't understand what the Revolution has meant to us. We owe all our accomplishments to Fidel."[6]

Many Castro loyalists also share Castro's Socialist views. According to Cuban American photographer Tony Mendoza, "Fidel's people are the socialist workers with plenty of *conciencia* [social conscience], those who volunteer in the cane fields, the government functionaries, the university professors, the military and the security people."[7]

Others may support the government, but do so primarily to advance their own interests. Many are ambitious individuals who wish to enjoy the wealth, power, and prestige that

awaits those who actively work to attain Castro's goals. They know that to gain such rewards they must above all else be active and loyal members of Cuba's Communist Party. Party membership is necessary for admission into Cuba's universities and to obtain better jobs. Those loyal to Castro are also more likely to be allowed to travel abroad, and they can shop in well-stocked stores reserved for party members. The benefits of party membership are not lost on ordinary Cubans, who often have little respect for those in the party. Says a twenty-eight-year-old Cuban exile, who prefers to be known only as "Omar," of the governing elite, "The people who live close to Fidel and work around him have a good life; they have no reason to have anything against Fidel. [If something bad happens] they let it go . . . they save their own skin."[8]

There are also other Cubans who work within the government and the Communist

Party but who no longer believe in the revolution. Such individuals do not criticize the power structure to which they owe their jobs and livelihoods. Instead, they go through the motions of supporting a political system they privately have lost faith in. Ordinary Cubans describe such government officials, who say one thing but do another, as having a *doble moral* (or dual morality). Numerous Cubans do what is expected of them. They feel powerless and never challenge the authorities, especially when faced with the real dangers of severe punishment.

Afraid of Change

The threat of reprisal, arrest, and bodily harm are not the only things keeping Cubans from speaking out against Castro. His control of the country is also made possible because many Cubans are afraid of change. Older Cubans, recalling how much worse their lives were before the revolution, dread losing what they have gained; younger Cubans know only life under communism and fear the unknown.

Not only are Cubans reluctant to risk what they have gained, they are often in the dark about what the alternatives are. Most citizens, no matter what their age, know only what the state tells them. What they hear over and over is that Cuba is a good place and that life elsewhere—especially in the United States—is wicked and dangerous. Because the government controls the mass media, as well as access to fax machines, computers, and the Internet, Cubans have few opportunities to compare reality with what their government tells them.

Castro also uses scare tactics to convince the Cuban populace that change could be dangerous. He repeatedly warns his country that if he were no longer in power, Cuban

"criminals" living in the United States—Castro's term for Cuban exiles—along with imperialist American politicians and greedy businessmen, would invade Cuba and take it over. In fact, the state routinely prepares Cubans for a possible invasion by the United States. In *Cuba Diaries: An American Housewife in Havana*, Isadora Tattlin recalls the siren alerts she heard in her Havana neighborhood, "It's like an old-fashioned siren, the one you crank. The *norteamericano* [North Americans'] invasion siren, which they test once a month, sounds more high tech. It's like moaning, too, and a muezzin [a Muslim prayer caller] calling worshippers to prayer. Rising and falling, and at the end, snarl-moans and rustling bushes."[9] Fear of the exiles and the United States makes many Cubans extremely anxious. Though many dislike their government, they also fear that an end to Castro's brand of communism would bring them nothing but disaster and chaos.

Finally, some Cubans support Castro's revolution, but not because it has created a prosperous, just society. Instead, they think Castro has built a society that keeps the worst from happening to people. According to journalist Christopher Hunt, Cubans know that Cuba is "the only country in the world where a person could do nothing, absolutely nothing, and not starve to death. Blanketed by security, many were afraid of the real world."[10]

A Future Without Hope

Castro's critics—both those who speak out at great personal risk and those who live in exile—admit that Castro has achieved limited success in education and medicine but say that he has largely failed to create a just, fair, and prosperous society for the Cuban people. Even worse, they say, Castro and

As a young employee at a Postal Savings Bank in Cuba, Armando Valladares had on occasions spoken out against communism in the early days of the Cuban revolution because it conflicted with his religious beliefs. For this offense he was arrested and imprisoned for twenty-two years. Upon his release in 1982, he reflected on the horrors he had seen as an inmate. The following extract comes from his memoirs, *Against All Hope*.

"As the cars sped along, a flood of memories rushed over me. Twenty-two years in jail. I recalled the two sergeants, Porfirio and Matanzas, plunging their bayonets in Ernest Diaz Madruga's body; Roberto Lopez Chavez dying in a cell, calling for water, the guards urinating over his face and in his gasping mouth; Boitel, denied water too, after more than fifty days on hunger strike, because Castro wanted him dead; Clara, Boitel's poor mother, beaten by Lieutenant Abad in a Political Police station just because she wanted to find out where her son was buried. I remembered Carrion, shot in the leg, telling Jaguey not to shoot, and Jaguey mercilessly, heartlessly, shooting him in the back; the officers who threatened family members if they cried at a funeral.

I remembered Estebita and Piri dying in blackout cells, the victims of biological experimentation: Diosdado Aquit, Chin Tan, Eddy Molina, and so many others murdered in the forced-labor fields, quarries, and camps. A legion of specters, naked, crippled, hobbling and crawling through my mind, and the hundreds of men wounded and mutilated in the horrifying searches. Dynamite. Drawer cells. Eduardo Capote's fingers chopped off by a machete. Concentration camps. Tortures, women beaten, soldiers pushing prisoners' heads into a lake of . . . [human manure], the beatings of Eloy and Izaquirre. Martin Perez with his testicles destroyed by bullets. Robertico weeping for his mother.

And in the midst of that apocalyptic vision of the most dreadful and horrifying moments in my life, in the midst of the gray, ashy dust and the orgy of beatings and blood, prisoners beaten to the ground, a man emerged, the skeletal figure of a man wasted by hunger with white hair, blazing blue eyes, and a heart overflowing with love, raising his arms to the invisible heaven and pleading for mercy for his executioners. 'Forgive them, Father, for they know not what they do.' And a burst of machine-gun fire ripping open his breast."

the pervasive intrusion of his government into every corner of daily life have prevented the Cuban people from finding solutions to their country's many social and economic problems. By now many Cubans realize that the United States is not mostly responsible for Cuba's current problems, as Castro claims. Instead, they understand all too well that their own government is the biggest obstacle to a better life. Many older Cubans who once took part in the revolution with a sense of optimism now believe their hard work and patience will not reward them. Younger Cubans who know life only through the stifling oppression of authoritarian rule have nothing to compare their lives to. Nor do they expect to have a chance to rise, unless they compromise their talent and integrity and become hacks for the Communist Party. According to Catherine Moses, who in recent years worked at the U.S. special interest office maintained by the Swiss embassy in Havana:

> Cubans in their twenties and thirties have experienced nothing but the Revolution, and they are less than enamored of it. These young people see no future in Cuba because they see no way to make a living under the current system, and they cannot imagine political or economic change occurring. They do not really have a sense of what being Cuban means besides what the Soviets and Fidel have force-fed them. For them, Cuba, the *patria* [fatherland], has been limited to socialism, and socialism to Fidel.[11]

For the time being, then, these young adults and all others in Cuba have little choice but to escape Cuba or remain and do the best they can to survive the daily challenges of modern life. And for most people, this is not easy to do.

Getting By in Castro's Cuba: *No Es Fácil* (It Is Not Easy)

Castro came to power pledging to provide the basic necessities for life to all Cubans fairly and equally. However, beginning in the early 1990s, things went badly for Cuba. As a result, no longer can the government make good on its promises.

No Es Fácil

Many Cubans face each new day unsure of how they will provide enough food for themselves and their families. Nor do they know how they will obtain medicine if they or family members fall ill. Money to buy adequate clothing is hard to come by. In talking about earning a living, Cubans can only shake their heads and tell one another, *"No es fácil"* (It is not easy).

Though there are many factors that contributed to this dire situation, the greatest one was the breakup of Cuba's biggest ally, the Soviet Union, in 1991. The Soviets had provided economic support to Cuba in the form of guaranteed purchases of Cuban sugar, various monetary grants, and large discounts on commodities such as petroleum. This aid quickly dwindled as the Soviet Union, beset with economic problems, disintegrated. Serious economic decline followed in Cuba, resulting in widespread misery. In addition, sugar prices fell throughout the world because of an oversupply, meaning that Cuba got even less money for its biggest export.

Fidel Castro responded to the loss of Soviet aid by cutting back many government services. To compensate for the loss of Soviet economic aid, Castro also ordered his government to export many Cuban-made goods, resulting in shortages of products that would otherwise have been available for Cubans to buy. Ordinary items such as lightbulbs and auto parts became hard to find. Many food items and medicines were also scarce. Castro tried to prepare his people for these hardships by announcing that Cuba had entered a Tiempo Especial (Special Time) that required Cubans to make personal sacrifices, as if they were at war.

Enduring the Special Time

The worst of these hard times occurred in the late 1990s Though conditions improved slightly in the early years of the twenty-first century, the lack of food, medicine, and other necessities remains a big problem in Cuba. The Cuban government rations food and other items to the Cuban people to meet their basic needs, as determined by their age and the number of people in each family. Cubans must present their ration cards to different government officials at different locations— one card for a bunlike piece of bread, another for dry goods such as cloth and ready-to-wear clothing, still another for certain vegetables, rice, beans, coffee, and lard. Candles, matches, and kerosene needed by families to provide light for their homes during the country's many power outages are also rationed. At times, only children up to seven years of age receive a daily milk ration. Others may have to make do with powdered milk, if they can find it. Because older children often must do without milk, they often suffer physically from a lack of calcium and vitamin D.

Despite the rationing, Cubans can never be certain that a particular product they want will be available. Often they discover that what they want to buy is sold out. Because their ration cards often limit the purchase of a particular item to only one out of thirty days, some customers then may have to wait up to a month for another chance to get a loaf of bread or a container of milk. Nonetheless, most Cubans have no choice but to wait in lines and hope for the best. Sometimes the wait in line can last for hours, so family members often take turns standing in lines.

The food shortage especially shocks Cubans old enough to remember prerevolutionary days, when food was abundant. Notes "Angelica," who left Cuba in the early 1960s when she was fifteen and who recently returned to Cuba to revisit the land of her youth:

> It was really shocking to see lack of food in a place where once you could, because of the weather, have two harvests; instead the fields were now lying fallow. That made me cry, not the sorry state of the buildings. I visited a relative and brought him things he asked me for such as toothbrushes, and shoes for his kids. He said that after he left work, he would go out and forage for food. That might mean finding a store that was selling whatever so they could make a meal out of it.[12]

To many Cubans, the long lines symbolize that the Cuban revolution is not living up to its promise of a better life. "Flora" (who does

To Have and Have Not

Catherine Moses is a U.S. official who lived in Cuba for two years. In her book *Real Life in Castro's Cuba*, she provides these observations on the qualities of the Cuban people that she believes allow them to endure hard times.

"The Cuban reality is painful. The constant struggle to get by economically drains people of energy. The political situation, with its constraints on expression and action, prevents individuals from changing their lives. The very survival of people in this environment seems surreal. How do Cubans face the adversity of each day? How have they survived watching the country they love fall to ruin? How have they confronted the bankruptcy of the Revolution and coped as they saw the better future they were building collapse? How do they go on, knowing there is no way out and possibly not even a way through?

The answer embodies, perhaps, the essence of being Cuban. Despite tremendous adversity, or because of it, the spirit of Cuba has survived and grown strong. The people of the island are bound together in a web of life. Friends and family make life bearable. People nurture and care for one another. Because material goods are scarce, most have learned that human niceties, such as a kind word or touch, are what is truly essential. These people have not merely survived; they continue to give one another love and have not lost their joy for life. This humanity and willingness to help one another have kept the society from falling apart."

not wish to use her real name because she fears retaliation by Cuban authorities against family members remaining there) grew up in a rural area of Cuba and is now a U.S. citizen, living in Florida. Because she makes periodic trips to visit relatives in Cuba, she can compare life in Cuba now to what she remembers of Cuba when she lived there as a youth: "The government says life is getting better but nothing's really getting done. People are now worse off than they were before the Special Time. People can't find items such as toilet paper. You have to swap pigs and food for clothes or female necessities."[13]

Simply getting to the government store can present a challenge. Because most Cubans earn little money, few are ever able to buy an automobile. Moreover, cars are scarce. Generally Cubans can own a car only if it was in their possession before the revolution. A few Cubans have a vehicle the state gave them as a reward for performing some vital task especially well. That means that most of the vehicles on Cuban streets are decades-old American-made vehicles or poorly built cars that were manufactured in the former Soviet Union and are at least ten years old. Even if Cubans have cars, constant gasoline shortages limit their driving. In response to such shortages, many Cubans walk to work or ride crowded government-owned buses and trucks. So severe is the lack of motorized transportation that bicyclists and passengers in horse-drawn wagons have become common sights in Cuban streets. In some cities horse-drawn carriages take children to school. Trains pulled by steam engines, some built at the dawn of the twentieth century, haul harvested farm products to market.

Even electricity is in short supply. Omar, who now lives in Florida, says, "Power shortages are common. The government has a schedule and rotates the shortages among the different regions of the country sometimes. They say it goes off for eight hours, but the power outage may last as long as 16 hours."[14]

Other resources are also in short supply, as American travel writer Christopher Hunt notes about his stay in the town of Santiago de Cuba:

To save energy, the city pumped water through the system just twice a week. The residents stored water for the dry days. Topless oil drums . . . [held the landlord's water reserves]. Worried about my ability to cope with Cuban austerity, he showed me how to flush the toilet and bathe with a bucket of water.[15]

Lack of adequate shelter also plagues Cuba. Tanja Sturm of the London-based World Markets Research Centre writes:

By the 1980s Cuba had a serious housing shortage and has since built virtually no new residential housing. Consequently, it is believed that some 15% of the country's housing stock is in poor condition, including some 1,000 houses that collapsed in the capital, Havana, in 1994 alone, and a further 4,000 that are still in a precarious state today.[16]

"Inventar, Resolver, y Escapar"

Many Cubans react to their nation's economic decline and the repression of the government with a determination to survive. Cubans are fond of saying that they display their will by trying to "inventar, resolver, y escapar" (be inventive, seek a solution to one's immediate problem, and then escape Cuba at the first

Many Cubans attempt to earn a living by operating bicycle taxies (right) that compete with government-operated buses (background).

opportunity). Armed with this folk wisdom, many Cubans do whatever they must in almost any situation to survive or to improve their lives. For example, since supplies of goods at government stores are often unreliable, people barter among themselves constantly. Cubans will exchange homemade soap, toothpaste, or cooking grease for a ride in a rusting truck to the dentist. Some set up their own informal, and often illegal, bus companies, driving truck cabs, towing broken-down buses, and charging passengers a few Cuban pesos for a ride. A few salvage or build spare parts for cars. *Resolver* describes "the juggling act by which a mother with a new baby will trade a dress for a hen to lay eggs, and then trade the eggs for goats' milk,"[17] writes journalist Eugen Linden.

Some Cubans attempt to make ends meet by selling items they have made or by moonlighting with a second or third job. Tomas, an unauthorized Havana taxi driver, who also serves as a guide and bodyguard, once told English travel writer Henry Shukman, "I'm three things."[18] The practice of *resolver* extends beyond being resourceful to include taking part in petty crime. For example, workers may steal items of value from their government-run workplace and sell them on a thriving black market that attracts shoppers who cannot find what they need in the official economy. Cuban economists think that during the worst of the Special Time Cubans may have spent as much as 50 percent of their income in the black market. Vendors appear daily on Cuban streets to sell items such as eggs, ice cream, and coffee that are often stolen from government warehouses. Lightbulbs disappear out of apartment hallways and end up on the street for sale. Despite their suspicions that street vendors are selling stolen merchandise, few Cubans condemn them for this. Most realize these sidewalk sellers are desperate. Indeed, stealing from the government is so widespread that it ceases to shock anyone. An estimated 40 percent of all produce harvested on certain Cuban fields every year may disappear, resulting in empty shelves in urban grocery stores. Independent Cuban Internet journalist Miquel Fernandez Martinez observes, "Someone said that no Cuban steals a million pesos but that a million Cubans steal one peso each."[19]

The fact that virtually all major economic enterprises and businesses in Cuba belong to the government can force people to engage in acts they might otherwise never commit. For example, some Cuban farmers reportedly will smash the legs of cattle, which belong to the state, and then claim the animal hurt itself by accident. If the inspectors verify that the animal is hopelessly injured and cannot be taken to market, it is slaughtered, and the farmers get to keep the beef for themselves. Says Cuban American Manuel Caberio, a teacher in Ocala, Florida, "A cousin of mine in Cuba says when the state-owned beer truck goes from one city to the next to make deliveries, people will go out into the streets with empty bottles and ask him to fill them up."[20]

Though many Cubans tolerate the thievery and black marketeering, the state is not so abiding. Cuban authorities have passed new laws that punish those who pilfer and waste government property with penalties of up to twenty years in prison.

Softening Socialism's Rules

Cuba's economic hard times have also prompted the government to make modest changes to its Socialist system. No longer does the Cuban government oppose all forms of private business. Today Cubans can choose from about one hundred government-approved *cuenta propia* (self-employment opportunities) to earn extra money. An estimated two hundred thousand Cubans now earn money from working in their own small businesses. In small shops and sidewalk stalls, they repair shoes, hawk trinkets to tourists, and sell fruits, baked goods, and drinks. Street musicians play guitars and bongos in hopes of earning tips from passersby. Young men and women prowl the streets looking for clients for travel and entertainment services and customers for family-run restaurants where traditional Cuban meals, consisting of chicken or pork, yucca (a tuber flavored with garlic), rice and black beans, plantains, avocado, and salad, are served.

These new entrepreneurs, however, are not allowed to become too successful. True to its Socialist doctrine, the Cuban government does not wish to see anyone become rich from private enterprise. To keep that from happening, the government may close the business down, or seize merchandise, money, or even consumer items the small-time merchants purchased with their earnings.

The government also restricts Cuba's experiment with free enterprise through taxes. For example, in 1993 a family-owned restaurant paid one hundred Cuban pesos a month in taxes. A year later, the government demanded one hundred U.S. *dollars* per month

A woman sells flowers on a street in the city of Trinidad. The Cuban government permits such small-scale entrepreneurship provided the business does not become too successful.

for the same tax. Two years later the tax increased to four hundred dollars. Many Cubans are angry and bewildered over the conflicting policies of their government, but there is little they can do. They understand that they may supplement their income through free enterprise, but they will never become rich as long as Castro is in power.

Mixed Economy

Allowing small-scale entrepreneurship is not the only economic concession the Cuban government has made in recent years. To bring in much needed foreign capital, Castro has also permitted the formation of *empresas mixtas* (joint business ventures) between the Cuban government and various corporations from capitalist countries. These joint ventures range from construction of tourist resorts to cement production and mining operations. Foreign firms are required to hire many Cubans as workers. Cubans actively seek these jobs because they pay as much as two and a half times what comparable jobs for Cuban enterprises pay. Workers also often receive fringe benefits from the foreign firms in the form of tips or luxury items such as soaps and shampoos. The Cuban government, however,

In his travel book *Mi Moto Fidel*, British motorcyclist Christopher P. Baker provides this sketch of everyday life on Havana's Calle Obispo (Obispo Street).

"Calle Obispo was steeped in Latin rhythms. Twangy guitar music and the measured clacking of *claves* [instruments consisting of two wooden sticks that are knocked together to produce a clacking sound] mingled with the chirp of bicycle bells, the tinny beating of tinkers' hammers, and the creak of decrepit jalousies swinging on rusty hinges in the brusque wind eddying in off the sea. Petty hawkers had set up their stalls on the sidewalks, selling peanuts, home-baked confections, small limes, and pomegranates shriveled like raisins. Every block had its puncture repairman (*'se reparan ponchera'*) and those eking out a living refilling cigarette lighters (*'se llena fosforera'*). They were part of Cuba's new small-time entrepreneurs, legalized in the summer of 1993 to save the country's rust-bucket economy from collapse. They touted their trade beneath timeworn buildings held up by nothing more than makeshift wooden braces.

We passed a 650 cc Norton Commando [a British-made motorcycle] from the 1960s parked on the sidewalk. True to form, it was dripping oil. A big-boned '57 Studebaker [American automobile] with voluptuousness tailor-made for pre-Castro Cuba forged its way through the narrow street like a square-rigged galleon. It was followed by a Russian Gaz jeep full of military figures in olive-green uniforms beeping a path through the crowd. Battered, high-finned relics of 1950s ostentation littered the side streets. Because of the gasoline shortage, many had been left to decay in the tropical heat and rain. They seemed a metaphor for the state of much of Habana Vieja [Old Havana], a 350-acre repository of castles and churches and columned mansions dating back centuries and boasting a spectacular amalgam of style . . . [ranging from eighteenth-century Spanish to nineteenth-century French rococo to 1920s art deco and others]."

once again makes sure that Cuban workers do not reap too much of a windfall. The government requires the foreign firms to pay their workers' wages in U.S. dollars directly to the Cuban government. It then pays the workers, but in Cuban pesos, which are worth far less than dollars. The balance stays in government coffers.

Working for U.S. Dollars

As a result of their government's policies, most Cubans earn very little from their full-time jobs. Average educated adults earn a monthly salary of about three hundred Cuban pesos, which is equivalent to about fifteen U.S. dollars. For most Cubans this means living on the edge of poverty.

A few fortunate Cubans are able to earn not Cuban pesos but U.S. dollars, which have greater spending power. Until recently the Cuban government forbade Cubans from even owning U.S. dollars. But the Special Time prompted Castro and government officials to make another exception to their previous policy. Under limited conditions, Cubans may earn dollars and spend them at special stores where goods are priced and sold in dollars.

But the extra buying power associated with dollars does not always make a big difference in people's standard of living. As one Cuban American living in Florida explains:

My family has a disabled relative still living in Cuba. Though she is an elderly woman and suffers from cancer, she receives very little money from the Cuban government. To get by, she cleans a house once a week and is paid only . . . 1 U.S. dollar. So, my mother sends her about $100 a year to help out. Sometime she sends food too. Once she sent some grits and told my relative that it goes well with eggs. A little while later she wrote my mother back: Next time please send an egg; they cost $1.50 a piece.[21]

Because the U.S. dollar is desirable, a second, parallel economy has developed in Cuba—one that relies on dollars, not pesos. When given a choice, some Cubans will refuse payment in their own national currency in favor of dollars, especially those from tourists.

Cuba's New Tourist Economy

Cubans earn U.S. dollars working for tips from foreign visitors in the growing state-controlled tourist industry at places such as historic old Havana Varadero Beach, or Playa Girón. The servers and managers at these tourist centers also earn Cuban pesos from the government and generally earn much more than Cuban doctors.

Although legitimate jobs in Cuba's tourist hotels are scarce, a large number of young

American tourists dine at an outdoor café in Havana. Cubans who work in the tourism industry often make more money than Cuban doctors.

Cuban prostitutes proposition a tourist on a Havana street. Although the practice is illegal, many women turn to prostitution to make ends meet.

Cuban women earn money illegally from the tourist trade. These women, called *jinterias*, provide sex to foreign tourists, many of whom come to Cuba for the sole purpose of obtaining sex partners. Some *jinterias* readily admit that they engage in prostitution to get money for makeup and stylish clothes or to gain access to nightclubs they could not otherwise afford. Others engage in prostitution simply because hard economic times leave them no choice. Many *jinterias*, in fact, come from good homes and are college educated. Some are trained in professions such as medicine and engineering but find that moonlighting as a prostitute provides them with enough extra money to buy nice clothes or to support their families and children. Often the families have no idea where the extra money is coming from. Sometimes, however, families fully support this illegal activity. The parents of some *jinterias* hope their daughters will marry a foreign tourist and escape Cuba forever.

Officially prostitution is against the law; Castro has condemned it, calling it morally decadent. Some observers, however, think that the state tolerates and perhaps quietly promotes Cuba as a tourist sex center. According to these individuals, the government sees prostitution as yet another way of giving employment to young women and bringing much needed foreign currency into the country. For their part, many Cubans are outraged that so many of their children and wives engage in what many consider a degrading activity just to survive.

Help from the United States

What many Cubans see as a less degrading way to acquire foreign currency, especially U.S. dollars, is to recieve financial gifts from relatives who have escaped Cuba and prospered. This transfer of wealth, which Cubans call *fulla*, began as a trickle when Castro allowed Cubans to own dollars and increased when U.S. president Bill Clinton relaxed travel restrictions on October 6, 1995. Following this change, a flood of exiles took the opportunity to visit their native Cuba. In addition to money, these visitors bore gifts of clothing, modern gadgets, and food. That influx of wealth continues. In fact, as much as $800 million now arrives in Cuba every year from exiled Cubans who want to share their prosperity with friends and relatives.

Observers believe that Castro permits this transfer of wealth in order to compensate for the loss of Soviet aid. Experts estimate that the influx of U.S. dollars far exceeds any revenue generated from Cuban sources. For many Cubans, both at home and in exile, the transfer of wealth also symbolizes the failure of Castro's Socialist experiment in Cuba, because even with financial help from abroad, Cuban society struggles to hold itself together.

Getting Along in Cuba: Social Structure and Human Relationships

Even though Castro's troops toppled Fulgencio Batista more than four decades ago, many Cubans still view the revolution as ongoing and unfinished and its goals as still achievable. In fact, they often refer to their society as "El Proceso" (The Process), the aim of which is to create better living conditions. According to Swedish social anthropologist Mona Rosendahl, who spent time in Cuba studying how people lived, "Leaders do not say that people have to sacrifice everything for their society but for the revolution. Proud citizens do not say 'look what we have achieved' but 'look what the revolution has given us.'"[22]

Prior to Castro's takeover of Cuba, the island had a rigid social system, dating back to the country's Spanish colonial period. A small, wealthy class of white landowners with strong ties to Spain ran the country. Cuba also had a prosperous middle class and a large number of illiterate poor people. Castro set out to restructure Cuban society to achieve equality and fairness for all people and to reduce the advantages once enjoyed by the ruling elite.

Today Castro's government forcefully— some say fanatically—continues to pursue this Socialist ideal. Under socialism the government runs most industries, businesses, power production facilities, and transportation systems. A dictatorship, Castro believes, is necessary to ensure that all these means of production function for the benefit of every-

one. According to Marxist-Leninist theory, to which Castro subscribes, the dictatorship eventually will wither away and leave a Communist society in which all citizens willingly share resources and work equitably.

Even critics of Castro and the tactics he employs admit that the state has taken great strides in ridding Cuba of many social and economic inequalities. For example, even the poorest Cuban has shelter, food, electric power, medical care, access to education, and a job. Because the state controls how much money an individual earns, the gap between the highest and lowest income groups is the smallest in all Latin America. The gap is also smaller than the income divide in the United States.

Social Leveling

The control over pay means that many Cuban professionals do not earn much more than workers; furthermore, they do not enjoy the high status their profession would bring them in most other countries. Observes journalist Eugen Linden, "Nowhere do people in elite professions such as medicine and science make less money than in Cuba. A physician typically earns no more than $100 a month. Bartering is common [for physicians]."[23]

However Cuban professionals may feel about their low pay and status, many others applaud the social leveling that the Cuban state has imposed. As Rosa Elena, a Bolivian who resided in Cuba, told author Mark Cramer, "In Cuba, even when cultural background is advantageous, professionals are considered at the same level as everyone else. It's this freedom from a system of social pretensions that I like about Cuba."[24]

Despite a mass of well-documented abuses by Castro's government, many Cubans are grateful for what the revolution has brought them. In fact, the degree of support a Cuban shows for the revolution often reflects how that individual is faring in Castro's Cuba compared to his or her circumstances before the revolution. Those whose lives have been greatly enriched by the revolution tend to support Castro and overlook government brutalities. As Juan, a resident of Santiago de Cuba, told author Christopher Hunt:

I feel rich. The cost of living in Cuba is very low. I own my home. Even if I didn't, the rent to the government is very low. I need only twenty pesos per month to buy food with the ration book. With my supplementary income I can buy extra food at the market. I don't have much money. But in the Cuban system, one doesn't need much money. I have everything I need.[25]

Because of the absence of an upper class and a middle class, Cubans tend to be free of both the snobbishness and the feeling of inferiority that haunt many other societies. As a result, Cubans tend to be outgoing and friendly with almost everyone they meet. They are quick to share what they have, even with strangers.

Before the revolution blacks and women of all races in Cuba suffered many forms of discrimination. Though problems remain, these groups have made many gains in employment and educational opportunities under socialism. Equality is also enshrined

Even critics of Castro acknowledge that his government provides even the poorest families with basic necessities such as food, shelter, and medical care.

While traveling through Cuba's countryside in a taxi, editor and author David Eggers observed a fleeting scene that seemed to symbolize Cuba's past, present, and uncertain future. This passage appears in Eggers's essay "Hitchhiker's Cuba" in Tom Miller's anthology titled *Cuba: True Stories*.

"Halfway to Trinidad, while we are passing La Guira, something recklessly symbolic happens. At the bottom of a small valley, there is a split second when a huge, bulbous green army truck passes us, heading in the other direction. At the same instant, we are passing on our right a straw-hatted framer on horseback and, to our left, a woman on a bicycle. Symbolism contained: each of our vehicles represents a different element of what makes Cuba Cuba. The bicycle is the Cubans' resourcefulness and symbiosis with their Communist brethren (about a million bikes were donated by the Chinese, a decade ago). The army truck is the constant (though relatively sedate and casual, we'd say) military presence. We are the tourists, perhaps the future, our dollars feeding into Cuba's increasingly dominant second economy, largely inaccessible to Cuba's proletariat; and the horseback farmer represents, of course, the country's rural backbone. All caught, for one split second, on a single linear plane."

in Cuba's constitution, a document that promises that all Cuban citizens are entitled to equal rights before the law. Defenders of modern Cuba insist that the state seeks to achieve equal justice, not equal salaries, for all Cubans.

There are others, however, who believe that the government's emphasis on equality has forced people to live in poverty. Castro's promise of equality "only ensured that everyone had nothing,"[26] asserts travel writer Lynn Darling.

Regardless of how they think about Castro and the revolution, many Cubans love their country and are disinclined to leave it. As anthropologist Mona Rosendahl observes, "Those who are loyal to the system believe Cuba is a good place to live *because* of socialism. Others feel that it's a good place to live *in spite* of the system."[27]

A Nation of Neighborhoods

As a rule, Cubans cherish their reputation for being friendly, sociable, and talkative. Some observers, in fact, think that Cubans talk all the time. The easiest place for Cubans to be convivial is in their neighborhood—with people they know very well. Author Mark Cramer observes, "Cuba is a country of neighborhoods. . . . Even a big metropolis like Havana is comprised of many smaller 'towns', with all the advantages of belonging to a social network and all the disadvantages of everyone knowing what you are doing."[28]

In their tight-knit neighborhoods Cubans enjoy a strong sense of community. Most Cuban families send their children to the same schools as their neighbors do and have the same physician, located in the neighborhood. They elect their own local government-approved representatives in neighborhood elections. To outsiders used to a more impersonal society, such closeness appears attractive. Cramer writes, "They [Cubans] attend neighborhood forums and street festivals. Corner bars and parks become public gathering places. This is the old-fashioned sense of

Living in tight-knit neighborhoods gives most Cubans a strong sense of community that helps many to cope with the hardships of daily life.

community that seduces people from more modernized cultural settings to visit a place like Cuba."[29]

During her days in Havana working at the Swiss embassy's U.S. special interest office, Catherine Moses observed that these strong human relations serve Cubans well during their current period of adversity. She writes:

> In Cuba, the personal is very important. The first courtesy is to ask how someone is and not expect a one-word answer. Individuals ask each other about their families and offer cups of coffee. Perhaps because there are no goods to buy and there are shortages of everything, people have learned to give of themselves. Cubans visit one another. They just drop in. Meals are shared. Those who may not have food are welcomed at others' tables. The favor is repaid somehow. They are part of one another's lives.[30]

To help one another, Cubans also often use *sociolismo* (the buddy system)—an informal network of personal relationships—not to be confused with *socialismo* (socialism), the political theory on which Castro's regime is based. Under the buddy system Cubans may help one another obtain hard-to-find car parts, or extra food for a party, or overnight lodging for friends or paying clients. They may also depend on friendships to keep the local Committee for the Defense of the Revolution spies and other government officials from interfering too much in the affairs of the small businesses or restaurants they operate in their homes. *Sociolismo* operates among state officials too. Many Cubans suspect that Communist Party members provide one another with special favors and secret information that is often withheld from the general population. For example, medical writer

Miquel A. Faria Jr., MD, notes that for a few Cuban doctors, such as those who are party members, *sociolismo* gets them foreign travel permits and assignments to clinics that treat foreigners.

Grouping for the Government

To a considerable extent the government encourages—and sometimes demands—that Cubans participate in organized group activities designed to serve society. Small brigades of university students, urban workers, and schoolchildren pour into Cuba's sugarcane fields for weeks at a time to help with harvesting. In return for their services, these so-called volunteers receive an *estimado* (a reward from the government). Often the reward is that a participant's name gets priority on a waiting list for an apartment. Or a luxury item, such as a refrigerator, may be provided by the government. Even young children are expected to serve by cleaning up or repairing their elementary schools. In addition, able-bodied Cubans gather in groups for military training for several days every month. Though the primary purpose of such training is to strengthen national defense, this compulsory activity also reinforces the Socialist goal of community and equality among Cuban citizens.

Family Life

For all the government's efforts to weave a cohesive society, the basic social unit in Cuba is the extended family. Though many Cubans marry and then divorce and live with unmarried partners, they still place a high value on family connections. "You can take a Cuban out of a family, but you can't take the family

Female volunteers help farmworkers weed a potato field. In return for their work, volunteers receive rewards from the government.

out of a Cuban" goes an old saying in Cuba. Relatives tend to live near one another. Because of housing shortages, as many as three generations often share an apartment or house.

The government's policy is to take on some of the roles that in the past were filled by family members. Notes Barbara Robson of the U.S. Refugee Program, many of the functions of the traditional Hispanic family have been "replaced by a reliance on day care centers and other public institutions. The community (neighborhood, church, school and production cooperative) also serves as something of an extended family, helping to reinforce social values and emotional security."[31]

As it does in so many other areas of everyday life, the Cuban government has a hand in determining what happens in families. Family planning, for example, is encouraged by the state. Birth control is widely practiced and women have easy access to legal abortions. Writes Mona Rosendahl:

Most younger Cuban women have had abortions, some as many as four. Sometimes the women have abortions instead of using contraceptives. If they get pregnant with a man with whom they do not want to live or when life is difficult, they get an abortion, which is free and available as long as there is no threat to the woman's life and she is less than twelve weeks pregnant.[32]

Government policies also affect families in that almost every Cuban family is divided by opinions its members have of Castro. Some family members may be enthusiastic "pro-Fidelistos," or supporters of Fidel Castro and his policies, which puts them at odds with "anti-Fidelistos." Sometimes husbands and wives divide over the issue, placing serious strains on the marriage.

The grim reality in Cuban society is that since the revolution began, between seven hundred thousand and 1 million Cubans have fled their native land, often leaving behind mothers, fathers, grandparents, sons, daughters, spouses, and other relatives whom they may never see again. Many Cubans are glad their loved ones live in freedom and prosper abroad, but they are also heartbroken that they are living in exile. They are also hurt if their loved ones forget about their family members in Cuba and do not support them with money and gifts from America.

Marriage and Divorce

One measure of the importance of family life to Cubans is the high rate of marriage in Cuba. In fact, in 1999 the country had the highest marriage rate in the world, with 17.7 per 1,000 people getting married each year. But unlike weddings elsewhere in Latin America, Cuban weddings are more likely to

Cuba has one of the world's highest marriage rates. More than half of the country's marriages, however, end in divorce.

be civil affairs. Church weddings in Cuba, in fact, are becoming rare.

Cubans are also likely to get married more than once in their lives, since more than half of all recent marriages in Cuba end in divorce. Every year about 4.2 people per 1,000 get a divorce, a rate that is slightly lower than that of the United States. Some observers think that lack of privacy resulting from people being forced to live in over-crowded homes may be a cause of divorce for many couples.

Women's Place in Society

Whatever effect government policies may be having on family life, there is no doubt that the revolution has fostered some basic changes in the way Cuban men and women relate to each other. Though elements of machismo—a deeply rooted belief in male superiority found in much of Latin America—still linger in Cuban society, Castro's Socialist government has done much to improve the status of women in recent decades. For example, women enjoy legal equality. They receive the same pay as their male counterparts. Sexual discrimination at the workplace is also illegal. Fifty percent of all Cuban university students and 60 percent of doctors are women. In addition, women serve in many positions of authority in the Cuban military. Women workers are entitled to eighteen weeks of maternity leave. Cuban law also requires that husbands do half the housework. New mothers can choose to stay home with their child until the child is six months old and receive 60 percent of their salary. Or they can take one paid day each month to stay home with their child. Government-run day-care centers provide child care for women who work.

Overall, Cuba's revolution has done much to foster independence among women. As author Mark Cramer explains, "With basic necessities assured and equal access to professions, a Cuban woman is much less likely to remain in a bad marriage out of economic necessity as many of her unfortunate counterparts in other Latin American countries do."[33]

Nonetheless, traditional attitudes about the roles of women and men die hard. Many Cubans view a man's ideal role to be *en la calle* (in the street), meaning that he is expected to be involved in public life and support his family by working outside the home. A woman's ideal role in the mind of many traditionalists is *en la casa* (in the house). This idea no longer means that women are expected to be confined to the home, but it does signify that many Cubans identify women with homemaking and child rearing, even though they may work full-time outside the home.

Race Relations

Just as the revolution has affected relations between men and women, so too has it affected race relations. A commitment to racial equality is enshrined in the Cuban constitution, which outlaws discrimination "by reason of sex, race, color, or class."[34] Before the revolution, Cuban blacks suffered widespread racial discrimination. Blacks were routinely excluded from many clubs, theaters, hotels, and schools. Cuban blacks were also denied admission to many occupations and social organizations. Castro abolished most of these prohibitions, paving the way for blacks to enter the mainstream of Cuban life. Today many blacks hold positions in the skilled trades and the professions.

Desperate Times for Cuban Women

In the following excerpt from *Afro-Cuban Voices: On Race and Identity in Contemporary Cuba*, Georgina Herrera, a black poet in Cuba, observes that blacks, and especially black women, have lost many of the economic gains they had made earlier in the Cuban revolution and have turned to prostitution to survive.

"Ever since Cuba has been Cuba there have been blacks and whites in our country. The whites always had the power, have always been better placed. Those who left Cuba at the start of the revolution because they had everything to lose were the whites. The blacks stayed. Now, whites are the ones abroad who can help their families—because now it's allowed, they're no longer traitors, or anything like that. Blacks are still the most marginalized, despite all the possibilities they have had. We laugh sometimes when we hear that a family member has sent for so-and-so because the relatives have died and there's an inheritance. The whites still get their inheritances, and all the blacks have is that they went to die in African countries because they're blacks.

So it's logical that blacks still face more economic privation, and, in the case of the black woman, who is also exotic and attractive, she has the most difficulties. Whites help each other out a lot. With the bankruptcy of the socialist camp [Cuban economy], chains of stores were opened that we call 'shoppings,' because you can only buy there in dollars, and all the whites who were in power in government started placing their people, their families and friends, and almost no black women. And so black women were the first to go into jiniterismo (prostitution). Needs aside, they know they're attractive. It's a means of survival, there's no doubt about that. . . .

All this started very sportily, but then grew tremendously when girls saw that others could get food, clothing, and shoes with the foreigners who come to Cuba, in exchange for sexual favors.

The phenomenon has spread like the plague, especially in the cities and in the major tourist attractions."

Despite these improvements, some observers charge that Castro has not gone far enough. They point out, for example, that few blacks have positions in the highest levels of government or the Communist Party. Many neighborhoods in Cuba are still largely racially segregated. Black youths often complain that Cuba's police harass them because of their color. Many blacks also grumble that Castro and his regime take black support for granted and expect everlasting gratitude and loyalty from blacks as payment for their newfound rights.

A Cherished Sense of Cuban-ness

No matter what race or color Cubans are, most have a strong sense of *Cubanidad* ("Cuban-ness"). Black or white, Cubans share a language and culture. This sense of shared cultural identity has proven a boon to Castro. "It is a major factor in the relative stability of the revolutionary government in Cuba,"[35] observes Barbara Robson.

Being Cuban also means something different today than it did before the revolution.

After decades of indoctrination, Cuba is now a society in which most Cubans, even those who hate Castro, have adopted values that set them apart from Cubans from an earlier time. For the most part, Cubans, especially those born after the revolution, believe that medical care, education, guaranteed employment, and housing for all are basic rights. Many also believe that it is the duty of the state to provide these things, even if it means allowing the state to curtail personal freedoms in return.

Communist-Style Inequality

Despite the sweeping changes in society, inequality does exist in Cuba. Instead of Cubans being advantaged because of race or wealth, under Castro a system has developed

Although deeply rooted sexism continues to exist in Cuba, women enjoy legal equality with men. Sexual discrimination is illegal, and women receive equal pay.

An experienced traveler in Cuba, British-born Christopher P. Baker explains in this section from his latest book, *Mi Moto Fidel*, his growing disenchantment with Castro's revolution and his conviction that the revolution is harming Cubans.

"On earlier visits to Cuba, I had felt sublime elation the entire time I was there. Havana still satisfied my soul, but this time around the island seemed to have lost much of its magic. At first, I thought I was becoming blasé about its unique enchantments, its genuine uplifting achievements. Then I realized I had seen through *el manto*—the mystical, otherworldly enigmas, the deception that Castro uses in pursuit of his cause. . . .

It wasn't simply a matter of Castro's . . . [stingy-unselfish dual nature], or the oppressive limitations on an individual's freedom to live the life he or she chose. For all the wonderful care it provided for the aged and the indigent [poor], the Cuban state was also robbing its own—requiring, for example, that Cuba's foreign hotel partners pay the government $450 monthly for each Cuban worker, who saw none of it; instead, they received worthless pesos from the state. I met a model who received five bottles of rum in lieu of a monthly salary, and a destitute elderly couple forced to sell the family gold and silver to the Cuban government for a fraction of its true worth. Another friend, refusing the state's paltry offer for a treasured family heirloom worth many thousands, had been threatened with its confiscation; the work of art, claimed the corrupt city official, belonged to Cuba's patrimony [heritage]. Some Cubans saw these indignities as necessary sacrifices on behalf of the Revolution. Most expressed deepening bitterness; their idealism seemed betrayed by power, corruption, and lies."

in which the politically connected get privileges ordinary Cubans can never hope for. Unlike most other Cubans, Communist Party members and their families enjoy a higher status than most of the populace. Leading party members are entitled to shop in special stores that offer an abundance of products not found in most peso or even dollar stores. They can travel abroad more easily than others and enjoy other privileges denied to ordinary Cubans. Next come the lower-ranking, faithful members of the party who are rewarded for their loyalty with special favors and privileges. Says Marti Walstad of Rome, Georgia, who recently traveled on a National Geographic expedition to Cuba, "Cuba has two classes: the poor and Castro's cronies."[36]

Cuba is also witnessing the rise of a relatively new class of people—those who, despite Castro's efforts to control them, manage to prosper in the dollar economy. This social class challenges the whole premise of equality that Cuba's Socialist society is based upon. Their newfound ability to earn dollars or to receive generous monetary gift from relatives in the United States divides members of this class from those at the bottom of Cuba's social structure—the nation's majority, who must scramble for a living in the peso economy.

Social scientists have noted the growing rift in Cuban society, one that goes beyond money itself to include how the money is acquired. Mona Rosendahl notes, "It is obvious to people today that not everyone has equal opportunities. Ownership of dollars is the clearest dividing line, but the opportunity to be self-employed is also critical."[37] Unlike their counterparts in Cuba's small but growing market economy, state employees must accept wages and salaries that are dictated by the state and are in the form of pesos, a currency whose spending power is weak compared to that of the dollar. As these workers face economic stagnation, a new class of Cubans, those enriched by *fulla* from Miami, along with those who benefit from tourist prostitution and black marketeering, are rising above them economically. As a sense of solidarity that comes from shared poverty and repression diminishes, some observers think that Cuba's very social structure is being undermined.

4 Literacy for All, Castro Style

Whatever their misgivings might be about other aspects of their society, many Cubans take immense pride in their educational system. It has produced a high number of university graduates and highly skilled workers and has created a citizenry of well-read people. "In general, Cubans are knowledgeable, often displaying an astounding level of intellectual development and erudition. Their conversations are spiced with literary allusions and historical references,"[38] writes Christopher Baker.

Cuba's educational system was not always so commendable. When Castro came to power, an estimated 27 percent of the Cuban people could not read or write. Good schools and teachers were rare. Much of the best education was available at private schools for the elite and at Catholic-run institutions. Even when schooling was available to the poor, many children in remote areas could not take advantage of them because they had to work in the sugarcane fields to help support their families.

Cuba's lack of schools was only one of Castro's problems concerning education when he came to power. The country's population of educated people dropped during the early days of the revolution, when thousands of Cuba's wealthy people—who were also the best educated—left the country, fearing a Communist takeover. In response to these challenges, Castro's revolutionary government launched a nationwide literacy and education campaign. In 1961 the state dispatched 120,000 people of all ages to teach reading

across the country, even in the most remote areas. The government also built ten thousand new classrooms, including many in rural areas that were in desperate need of schools. If officials believed building new schools in a certain region was impractical, they arranged transportation for rural children to attend existing schools elsewhere.

These efforts paid off. Even Castro's harshest critics reluctantly admit that Cubans have benefited from the government's efforts. Today, the Cuban government boasts that 98.5 percent of Cubans are literate. Supporters of Cuba's educational system also point to a 1998 study by the United Nations Educational, Scientific and Cultural Organization (UNESCO) revealing that, despite the nation's current economic problems, third and fourth grade Cuban students outperformed most of their counterparts in Latin America in music and language on standardized tests. In fact, because the scores were so high, UNESCO officials became suspicious that the tests had not been administered correctly and retested the Cuban students. The second try revealed the same high results. Making such achievements even more remarkable is the fact that Cuba is one of the poorest countries in the world.

Training the "New Man" and the "New Woman"

Providing Cubans with basic literacy is just one function of the nation's educational system. Indeed, the top priority for schools is to indoctrinate students with Castro's brand of socialism. Across Cuba youngsters learn the revolutionary message: *Estudiantes hoy, trabajadores mañana, soldados de la patria siempre* (Students today, workers tomorrow, soldiers of the nation always).

This indoctrination effort began during the early days of the revolution, when Castro decided to overhaul Cuba's school systems and fashion them along the lines of the Communist model used in the Soviet Union, which at the time was the world's leading Communist power. "The concept is to use education as an instrument to create a new man, whose god is revolution,"[39] says Luis Zúñiga, director of the human rights division of the Cuban American National Foundation.

Today that revolutionary educational philosophy remains very much in place. Schools in Cuba are expected to teach the value of loyalty to the country and the Communist Party, not to analyze or criticize them. At an early age, even Cuba's youngest students receive an educational and political indoctrination that are woven together. Their lessons stress important values associated with socialism, such as group work, unity, and equality. Cuban schools teach these communal values by "stressing group play, requiring students to care for the school grounds and farms, teaching vocational skills, and focusing on the development of a politically and morally 'correct' background on the part of each student,"[40] writes Barbara Robson of the U.S. Refugee Program.

Schools monitor how well students learn these political lessons. Officials maintain a dossier on each student, called the Cumulative Academic Record, that tracks their political

Cuba's educational system has improved greatly since Castro came to power. Today nearly 99 percent of Cuba's population is literate.

fitness for higher education and placement in society when they graduate. Any negative remark from a teacher about a student's attitude concerning Castro or the state could prevent that student from entering a university or from freely selecting a career.

As part of their Socialist training, students also learn that capitalism is bad and that socialism is good. They also learn that before the revolution life in Cuba was generally bad but that now it is much better because of the revolution and the hard work of its leaders, especially Fidel Castro. From an early age students are also taught that the Cuban way of life is one of the best in the world and that most of the economic and political systems to be found outside the country are inferior.

Molding of Minds Starts Early

Cuban children begin their political indoctrination at an early age. Elementary school students begin each school day by singing: "Pioneers for communism, we shall be like Che." This tribute is to Ernesto "Che" Guevara, an Argentine-born revolutionary who took part in the Cuban revolution and who was killed while attempting to foment a revolution in Bolivia. Today the Cuban government still promotes Che as a patriotic hero whom young people should honor and emulate.

Political indoctrination goes well beyond singing patriotic songs. Even reading lessons for elementary school students contain Socialist messages. Many first graders, for instance, learn to read from textbooks with sentences such as the following: "'F' stands for Felito. . . . Felito sharpens the 'mocha' (a short machete) and beside it, he places the 'fusil' (rifle)."[41] Such lessons are meant to emphasize to young children that what is important in

Cuban life is to honor Castro, study, and fight. According to Internet journalists Agustín Blázquez and Jaums Sutton, "Beginning in preschool, children are taught songs and poems praising the revolution and Castro, establishing a personality cult around his figure. Also, belief in God is discouraged. They are taught instead, to believe in Castro."[42]

Elementary school children are taught to denounce enemies of Castro and the revolution, especially the United States, a nation that allegedly is responsible for many of Cuba's problems. Many Cuban instructors also teach their pupils that American imperialism is a constant danger to Cubans and their way of life. Students are taught that the United States is poised to attack Cuba at any moment and that Cubans must be vigilant and prepared to fight when duty calls. Recalls fifteen-year-old "Julie," who attended school in Cuba, "We used to have evacuation drills twice a week to prepare for an attack. One time an airplane went over the school when we were having a drill and all the kids were afraid it was the Americans."[43]

Cuban schools require more than just learning about socialism and its enemies. All elementary school students must also become Pioneros (Pioneers), the Communist equivalent of the Boy Scouts and Girl Scouts. Pioneros, however, are also trained to be government watchdogs in their neighborhoods. Students are even encouraged to report any suspicions they might have of family members to government officials.

Young Cubans receive more of the same indoctrination when they attend middle and high schools. They start each school day singing political anthems or reciting speeches from revolutionary heroes. Among other things, they learn how to care for and use weapons. Political indoctrination continues at the university level. Not only must university

A Chance to Get Educated

Swedish anthropologist Mona Rosendahl in her book *Inside the Revolution: Everyday Life in Socialist Cuba* provides the recollections of a Cuban woman known only as Anita, born in 1947, who tells of her experience attending one of the special schools Castro created to teach rural children.

"My father did not want me to go to school in Havana, but I made an application myself to the Ana Betancourt school for peasant girls. That was a school directly run by the government for the education of women. I wanted to be a schoolteacher. I had always wanted that, and I thought that I did not learn anything at school here. We went to Havana by car, boat, and train. I had never been inside a car before, and of course not in a train. After that very tough journey, we came to Havana and they brought us to a house in Miramar that would be our hostel. That was like a dream. That rich house. I remember that we came in and there was beautiful furniture; there was everything, but we sat down on the floor, dead from fatigue. I will never forget that they gave us a little box with white rice and a steak. That was glorious. After that terrible journey. A revolutionary instructor, as they called them, came and took care of us. They gave us a test to determine which class we would go to, and I went to the first grade. But we were twelve, thirteen years old, so they accelerated the education. They taught us everything, everything. It's terrible that I have forgotten so much of what they taught us. They taught theater, dance, choir singing, playing instruments, and the teachers were really good. Every Sunday we went to the cinema or to the aquarium or some other place. We went to see plays, that play of Hamlet, and I did not understand anything then. They wanted to cram all culture into our heads, just like that, in one stroke. The century of ignorance that made us so backward, they wanted to take that away in no time."

students belong to the Communist Party, they also have to make sure that their academic pursuits never challenge or contradict official party positions. To do otherwise—for example, to write an essay critical of Castro—would ruin their academic careers.

Basic Schooling

Cuban students, however, receive much more than political indoctrination at school. They also get basic schooling in academic subjects. Education is free and available to all in Cuba. Dressed in school uniforms, students attend one year of preschool, six years in primary school, and another six at the secondary level. Education is mandatory until the age of fifteen. Cuban students receive instruction in literature, math, science, language arts, and social sciences, much as their counterparts do in many other countries. In response to growth in Cuba's tourist industry, many students also focus on English to prepare them for jobs that require direct contact with growing numbers of tourists from Europe, where English is widely spoken as a second language.

Cuban's educational system also seeks to instill in students a strong work ethic. During the first three years of secondary school, many students are required to go to special

Pioneers (Cuba's equivalent of the Boy Scouts) salute the Cuban flag. All elementary school students must become Pioneers, who serve as government watchdogs in their neighborhoods.

country schools. There they work for three hours in the morning at state-run farms—usually sugar or tobacco plantations—and attend classes the rest of the day. School authorities claim the work experience helps mold students into good workers. In addition, the free labor provided by the students helps to defray the cost of their education. But critics argue that children should not be used as a source of free labor. They also charge that the state uses the schools to diminish the influence of parents and replace it with that of the government as it seeks to mold students into young Socialists.

For their part, many Cuban parents hate these country schools. Some believe their children are too young to be sent away from their families. They are also distressed be-cause of the schools' reputation for what they consider moral laxity. Young teens of both sexes live in close proximity to one another at the schools, where there is little adult supervision. As a result, some parents say, many become sexually active at an early age. These sexual adventures often lead to unwanted pregnancies and the spread of sexually transmitted diseases. Some observers of Cuban society suggest that these premarital sexual experiences contribute to a high level of promiscuity among Cuban teenagers and adults. Some critics also suggest that sexual experimentation at the country schools may indirectly contribute to the rising numbers of *jinterias*, young prostitutes who ply their trade in the state-run tourist industry.

During their last three years at the secondary level, students specialize, attending either academic high schools or vocational schools that combine study and on-the-job training in factories. Gifted athletes may also enroll in special sports schools that provide training for Cuba's successful sports programs. Still other students with artistic interests enroll in arts schools.

Higher Education

Upon completion of high school, all students must first serve one year in the military or perform some sort of public service work before going on to university or trade school. Avoidance of this duty is almost impossible. Once they have fulfilled that obligation, about 17.2 percent of all Cuban high school students go on to attend one of Cuba's four universities.

Under Castro's regime, no student has a right to enter a Cuban university by high academic achievement alone, as was the case before the dictator took power. Instead, state authorities consider acceptance to a university as a privilege based on both academic achievement and the level of loyalty the student has demonstrated to the revolution and Cuba's Communist Party. These requirements mean that students who expect to succeed at the university level must join Communist-affiliated organizations and

Students work on a state-run farm during part of their school day. The state believes that using students as a source of labor helps defray the cost of their education.

support the government and the party line at every step of their academic careers. In fact, admission to a Cuban university is based in part on how well students do on an entrance test that reveals their "revolutionary attitude."

The government makes it clear that anyone expressing antirevolutionary or anti-Castro sentiments will be banned from attending any of Cuba's universities. Critics of the Cuban educational system claim that some college-bound high school students were denied entry into a university because they held unpopular political views or refused to publicly denounce their parents as enemies of the revolution. In addition, until recently, many students who openly professed a religious belief were also turned away.

If they are accepted, Cuban students receive a free university education. But this benefit is offset by a lack of freedom in choosing a course of study and a subsequent career. Students may indicate their preference of a course of study, but the government has the final say on their area of specialization.

As is the case with elementary and secondary schooling, the university curriculum includes a strong political component. In addition to the basic courses in their specialized field, university students must take courses, such as scientific communism, that stress the Socialist goals of Cuba. Many of their academic courses also integrate instruction in socialism and communism.

Once students depart a university with a degree in a given field, they must work at a job in a state-designated location for a certain number of years to repay the government for its investment in their education. According to a U.S. State Department report, "This education is held over their heads and is used as a tool of moral obligation to produce conformity and acceptance of actions taken by the state. By being part of the system, one is con-

sidered to have forfeited any sense of 'free professionalism' or independent practice."[44]

An Oversupply of Graduates

Those who do make it to a Cuban university generally attain high levels of academic achievement as college students. In fact, because so many university students manage to complete the requirements of a degree, Cuba is overstocked with well-trained professionals, especially doctors, engineers, and scientists. Though Castro and his supporters are proud of this fact, critics charge that the surplus of professionals is a waste of talent, time, and money. They also argue that Cuba does not need so many highly trained people, because there is not enough work for them. Cuba, in fact, sends as many as half of the doctors it trains to foreign countries. Castro claims that these doctors serve a useful purpose by providing medical care for thousands of poor people, mainly in Latin America, who would otherwise not receive any help.

Regardless of the government's true intention, many of the country's abundance of professionals are fated to earn low wages and to do meaningless work in inefficient bureaucracies. Some will never find any work in their chosen profession and will have to accept employment for which they are overqualified. In fact, as a result of the lack of opportunity, Cuba is one of the few nations in the world where the middle class, largely made up of university graduates, lives in near poverty.

New Problems

Although Cuba's university system works all too well in turning out qualified graduates, its overall educational system faces new prob-

Thousands of teachers celebrate the start of the school year by waving Cuban flags. Cuba's labor pool suffers from an overabundance of well-trained professionals.

lems that affect the daily lives of students, parents, and teachers. The Special Time that followed the collapse of the Soviet Union also took its toll on Cuba's schools. The UN Economic Commission for Latin America and the Caribbean estimates that spending for Cuba's schools dropped 48 percent between 1989 and 1995. As a result of this shortfall, many Cuban schools fell into disrepair and neglect and have not yet fully rebounded. School and instructional materials have been in short supply. To resolve these problems school officials often must ask for handouts. Isadora Tattlin recalls the visit she received from officials of the Cuban school that her children attended:

The director of the school and an assistant come to our door this morning. The director tells us they need detergent, rags for cleaning the floor, disinfectant, a broom. There are little children in the school. She and the teachers are afraid for their health. They have had nothing to clean the school with for months.[45]

Even food services were affected during the Special Time. Recalls Julie, who is now a high school student in the United States, of her elementary school days in Cuba:

I remember vividly the bread at school was so hard and old that you could throw

A Misguided Educational System?

The following excerpted passage from Carlos Alberto Montaner's book Journey to the Heart of Cuba: Life as Fidel Castro *questions Castro's claim that Cuba's educational system is a success.*

"The Revolution has built many schools, but it did start out with one of the highest educational levels in Latin America. When Castro boasts of having ended illiteracy— 24% of the population . . . he hides the fact that in 1958 Cuba had proportionally fewer illiterates than Spain (and that was true since the end of the 19th century), and that the deficit was gradually being addressed. The same could be said of the school indexes. When the Revolution began, they were not satisfactory, but they were very close to Italy's, a fact that must not be overlooked, since development is always an exercise in comparisons and contrasts. In the field of education, in the 1950s, Cuba had problems and difficulties, of course; but there is one curious fact that is very eloquent. At that time, most of Latin America was using mainly textbooks written by Cuban professors and printed in Cuba. . . . That could only have been possible if Cuban educators had achieved an exemplary level of quality and professionalism.

The truth, however, is that education in Cuba has reached even the most remote corners of rural life, and the country today has a high proportion of university graduates. But this auspicious achievement—which obscures the fact that the education [has to conform with the ideas of those in authority] . . . [and is] full of censorship and prohibitions, indoctrinating students more than training them—also raises a question. How is it possible that a society that has so much human capital lives so miserably? How is it possible that so many engineers, economists, doctors and teachers haven't been able to construct a more prosperous society? Far from absolving the Revolution, this substantial human capital is what indicts it, this is what shows it to be a disaster as an economic system.

There is no country in the world, except Cuba, in which so many professionals sometimes go hungry or have to walk around in shoes that are in tatters."

it at a wall and it would bounce back. They would feed you old soup that had been in a pot for days. And it wasn't really soup; they threw bones in for flavoring. Sometimes, you did get scrambled eggs cut in pieces, but no spices, no oils. If you wanted any kind of oil or grease, you have to grow pigs, kill them yourself and take out the fat and use that.[46]

Adding to the schools' problems, many poorly paid teachers have left the classroom to seek more lucrative positions in Cuba's dollar economy as a way to *resolve* their economic needs. Their departure from the classroom means that school authorities are having a tougher time than ever recruiting qualified teachers into the educational system.

Intellectually Imprisoned

Despite its flaws, Cuba's educational system still earns praise from people around the world, especially when it is compared to many other Latin American school systems. But it also draws criticism. Some argue that although the Cuban government teaches its citizens how to read and write, it does not teach them how to think independently. Teachers, as a rule, do not teach their pupils to critique their government and its ability to deal with pressing social and economic problems. In fact, in some cases school and government authorities punish students when they do offer such criticisms.

Although Cuba has achieved high literacy and academic levels, many of its most gifted and educated citizens remain intellectually imprisoned. Many are frustrated that although they have developed an educated and cultured mind, they cannot use it to get ahead financially or to participate in the decision-making process in Cuban society. Critics of Cuba's government charge that by repressing its own intellectuals, the state hurts the nation, because the country's talented thinkers cannot honestly appraise Cuban society and suggest solutions to the country's many social, economic, and political problems. "One of the saddest elements of life in Cuba today is that there are thousands of educated thinkers held prisoners in their own minds—a hellish internal prison,"[47] writes Catherine Moses.

Making matters worse is the fact that numerous students conclude early on that a good education does not always pay off in Cuba. Increasingly, they find themselves in a society where prostitutes, black marketeers, and service workers in the tourist trade make more money than doctors, dentists, engineers, professors, and teachers. In response to such a system, many students abandon their studies and instead begin to hustle in Cuba's dollar economy as their elders do.

Trying to Stay Healthy

Like universal education, good medical care for all Cubans is a top priority for the Cuban government. And like the country's educational system, health care in Cuba is mostly free and available to all Cubans, regardless of their ability to pay. Until recently, even foreign visitors could enjoy the benefits of free medical services.

Creating a new health-care system in Cuba was not easy for the country's leaders. The exodus of professionals when Castro came to power included half of Cuba's doctors (about six thousand), along with many nurses. Their departure left the country's health-care system in a crisis. Despite this setback, Castro and his fellow revolutionaries were determined to improve the health of the Cuban people, especially the rural poor. Medical personnel rid the country of many communicable and parasitic diseases. They also vaccinated people and created a health-care system that provided basic care to all Cubans. Today leaders and medical experts around the world say Cuba's universal health-care system is one of the best in the world. Distinguished visitors from Great Britain, the United Nations, and other lands and organizations have all praised the Cuban system for its quality, affordability, and availability.

One measure of the success of Castro's system is that when he came to power in 1959 life expectancy for Cubans was forty-eight years for men and fifty-four for women. Today Cuban men on average can expect to live to age seventy-four, and women age seventy-

six. Cuba has a 100 percent immunization rate against diseases such as measles and polio. Health officials have also eliminated diseases such as malaria and diphtheria. Moreover, Cuba's infant mortality rate of just seven per one thousand births draws praise from observers worldwide. In 1959 Cuba had only one medical school; now it has twenty-one. Finally, supporters of the Socialist system credit Castro's regime with bringing universal, low-cost medical care to all Cubans. In a 2000 report the British National Health Service estimated that Cuba's health care costs about 7 British pounds ($11.52) per person a year, compared to Britain, where equivalent care costs 750 pounds ($1,235.34).

Critics—especially those among Cuba's exile community in the United States, who have firsthand experience in Cuba's health-care system—say such statistics do not tell the whole story. Some question the validity of the statistical information a totalitarian regime provides to the world community. The U.S. State Department also points out that Castro inherited a health-care system that already compared favorably with those of other Caribbean countries. In 1959, for example, Cuba's infant mortality rate was thirty-two per one thousand births. Though that rate is higher than today's figure, it was the lowest in Latin America at the time and the thirteenth lowest in the world.

Castro's detractors also say that Cuba's Socialist approach to health care has resulted in low-quality medical care, shortages, and inefficiency, which have gotten even worse during the Special Time. Moreover, they charge that Cuba is providing medical care to foreigners who visit the island at the expense of the Cuban people in order to raise money to keep a failed Socialist system afloat.

The Structure of Cuba's Health-Care System

Making money was never the primary intent of Cuba's health-care system, In fact, many creators of the system believed that medical care is a human right. They did not want a for-profit system like that found in the United States. Cuba's revolutionaries believed that the government has the moral responsibility of providing treatment, regardless of a person's ability to pay. Today, however, medical authorities find that in an area of shortages and budget cuts, providing universal care for Cubans puts the government in a bind. Using a state-run socialized health-care system also means that the state employs all health-care workers—doctors, nurses, technicians, researchers, pharmacists, administrators, and others. In addition, funding for almost all medical programs comes primarily from the government. For the most part, these services are free and universal to all Cubans. Cuban medicine, however, is only free in the sense that patients do not pay directly for

A team of Cuban surgeons performs surgery in a Havana hospital. Many credit Castro with introducing affordable health care for all Cubans.

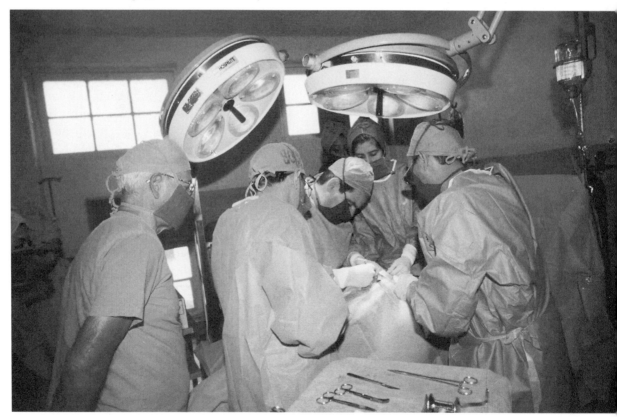

most services they receive. Instead, the Cuban government incurs these expenses with economic resources that belong to the Cuban people. Patients also must pay for medication.

Cuba's health-care system emphasizes prevention, health education, and community medical care. It also maintains medical facilities at the local, provincial, and national levels. The majority of Cubans receive most of their treatment at the local level under the Family Doctor Program. As part of this plan, doctors live and work at three-story buildings called *consultarios*, located in neighborhoods across Cuba. The clinic is on the first floor, the doctor and his or her family live on the second floor, and the nurse lives with his or her family on the third floor. Doctors are responsible for caring for 120 to 200 people who live in the immediate area.

The goal of these community-based clinics is to foster strong ties between doctors and their patients that in turn will result in the prevention of illness. Cubans are taught at an early age that they should stay healthy not only for their own benefit, but also because they have a duty as revolutionary citizens to avoid falling ill and becoming a burden to the state and their communities.

In addition to receiving primary medical care at their local *consultario*, Cubans visit their doctor twice a year for routine physical checkups, diagnostic medical tests, and immunizations. Patients also consult with doctors about any medical problems they may have and receive the latest government information about nutrition, exercise, medicine, prenatal care, and other health issues.

Neighborhood doctors are on call twenty-four hours a day. They also make house calls, especially whenever their patients are too ill to leave their homes or whenever they fail to show up for an appointment or treatment.

Hospitals and Polyclinics

When their patients have medical needs that cannot be provided at the local level, *consultario* physicians help them find a bed in a city, provincial, or national facility, depending on the type of care they need. Doctors can also rely on a backup network of laboratories, referral centers, and medical consultation services to aid them in providing comprehensive medical care.

Most towns also have specialty clinics, such as a maternity home and an adult care center for elderly people who, because of failing health, need supervision but whose children must work during the day. Many towns in Cuba also have facilities known as polyclinics, which house social services, emergency rooms, pediatrics, gynecology, and other medical services all under one roof. Advanced hospital care is also available at the polyclinics for those who need specialized treatments for cancer, heart disease, and other serious medical problems. In addition, Cuba has an abundance of highly trained physicians and surgeons available to perform advanced surgical procedures, such as organ and bone marrow transplants.

Success in Handling AIDS

Though its methods have been widely criticized, Cuba's health-care system has had great success in containing the AIDS epidemic, a problem that is a scourge in other countries. In fact, Cuba's HIV infection rate is one of the lowest in the world, and far lower than those of many of its Caribbean neighbors. This achievement is possible because Cuban medical authorities implemented a comprehensive AIDS prevention program. For more than twenty years the state has attempted to screen almost everyone in the country for the disease. Those who show signs of infection are forced to live apart from their families, friends, and loved ones in special sanitariums called *sidatorios*. There they receive counseling, food, housing, treatment with antiretroviral drugs, and other forms of government financial support. Though many of the severely infected live as virtual prisoners in these sanitariums and are considered victims of human rights violations by many outside observers, Cuban authorities believe their isolation is for the good of the entire society. "This permanent and obligatory quarantine is 'for the common good,' and those who oppose the quarantine practice are seen as 'enemies of the Revolution,'"[48] explains Barbara Robson.

Cuba's AIDS policy forces some families to make an agonizing choice: share barely adequate rations or part with a loved one. "A couple I met on a recent trip to Cuba has a 22-year-old son who has to hide with his parents because he has AIDS . . . and they don't want him taken away," says an American woman who recently visited Cuba. "Now the parents have to forage for three, when they only have rations for two."[49]

Fear of being quarantined may be lessening, however. American experts who study Cuban medicine report that in recent months Cuban authorities have begun to ease restrictions and have allowed some patients who have been counseled about the way AIDS is transmitted and the importance of safe sex to leave the sanitariums for home visits. Though many patients are eager to leave, others prefer to stay. According to Dr. Byron Barksdale, a pathologist in North Platte, Nebraska, and the director of the Cuba AIDS Project, about half the patients decide to stay because the sanitarium provides food, shelter, medicine, privacy, and other services—all of which

would otherwise be difficult to obtain outside the institution.

For the moment, Cuba's health-care providers seem to have the spread of AIDS under control. But many authorities worry that this success may be undermined by the heavy Cuban involvement in the lucrative tourist sex industry.

Health-Care Troubles on the Rise

Meanwhile, Cuba's much vaunted health-care system is facing serious challenges. One such challenge is that the demand for medical services has increased at the same time that the availability of medical resources has decreased. This situation is a result of problems brought on by the Special Time.

Many health problems are directly attributable to the hard economic times that followed the evaporation of Soviet economic assistance. For example, neuritis, a condition caused by vitamin deficiencies, became prevalent as breakdowns in food distribution systems meant that Cubans no longer had a balanced diet. Tanja Sturm, a writer with the London-based World Markets Research Centre, writes, "Poor nutrition and worsening housing and sanitary conditions have been associated with a rising incidence of tuberculosis—from 5.5 cases per 100,000 population in 1990 to 18.0 per 100,000 in 1997 (latest figure available)."[50] Beriberi, a disease caused by a lack of vitamin D, is also on the rise.

Cuba's Special Time has contributed to health problems in other ways. Because garbage pickups declined as a result of reduced government services, the rat population has increased, especially in the big cities, causing a rise in leptospirosis, a disease spread by contact with the rodents' feces.

An AIDS patient (left) and her family sit on the porch of a sanitarium outside Havana. Cuba controls the spread of the disease by forcing those with HIV to live in isolation.

Even good intentions have added to Cuba's health problems. The world's largest Communist-led nation, China, donated 2 million bicycles to Cuba at the start of the Special Time to help alleviate transportation problems. Riding these vehicles might have been expected to boost the health of Cubans by reducing heart disease. Instead, because so many Cubans had reduced their intake of food at the same time they were burning up more calories by bicycling, people suffered even more from inadequate nutrition. Says Cuban psychiatrist Marcos Dmaz Mastellari, MD, "People were walking or riding bicycles for miles on little or no food to get to and from work. We are still dealing with the neuropathies that developed in large sectors of the population at that time."[51]

Hunger and malnutrition have taken their toll, but so has the stress from the daily chore of finding enough food and drink. Doctors report an increase in stress-related health problems. According to travel author Christopher Hunt, in recent years suicide in Cuba has moved up from being the seventh most common cause of death to the fourth or fifth most common cause.

Environmental problems also contribute to poor health in Cuba. Gasoline shortages have removed many cars from Cuban highways and forced people to walk and ride bicycles. Any health benefits from these developments are offset by the presence of fleets of old cars that are in poor repair and therefore pollute the air, causing respiratory problems.

Adding to Cuba's health woes is the other major impact from the Special Time on Cuba's health-care system: The country's economic decline also meant that people were unable to purchase medical supplies, medicines, and other resources just when they needed them most.

The Weakening of Cuba's Medical Infrastructure

Because of the nation's economic problems, hospitals have become rundown and unsanitary. Doctors lack antibiotic soap, disinfectants, and medicines. Antibiotics and even bandages are in short supply. "We don't even have enough disposable syringes, so we have to sterilize them and reserve them for HIV patients and for those with hepatitis B and C,"[52] says Nadilia Ramos Bernal, a nurse who works in a *consultario* in the valley of Vinales in Cuba.

Infections after surgery and childbirth are on the rise. Physicians write prescriptions for their patients, but all too often the medicines are not available, because Cuba cannot afford to produce or import them. Even aspirin is

A Cuban Journalist Bemoans His Country's Health-Care System

In this excerpt from his online article "Public Healthcare in Cuba: A Challenge for the Future," independent Cuban journalist Oswaldo de Cespedes expresses anguish for the troubles facing his nation's health-care system.

"For those who haven't been to Cuba or people visiting the Island on pleasure trips, the numbers and the good propaganda they are fed may dull their brains and cause them to believe that Cuba is the Babylon of the Caribbean. But we who live here and daily struggle with a suffocating lifestyle, we know that in this 40-year struggle we have lost the city walls and the gardens, and that only ruins remain of what once was known as the Pearl of the Antilles.

The concept of health is a very broad one and includes not only the biological order of the human being but, by definition, health is the complete biological, psychological and sociological well being of the individual. In other words, the psychological and sociological aspects must be added, inasmuch as the environment and living conditions impact directly on the quality of life of the individual, which is the main objective of a healthcare system.

If we limit the definition of health to a decrease in child mortality, longer life expectancy, primary healthcare, and the creation of research and biotechnological institutes, then Cuba is the image of socialist success. However, if we talk about the real meaning of health and delve into all of the aspects that affect man as a social being, then there is no health in Cuba, and the degradation in the quality of life of the Cuban people is the only thing that socialism has achieved.

To confirm this, just visit any Havana neighborhood, walk through any back street, note the unsanitary conditions surrounding the population due to the shortage of running water, the accumulation of waste and debris, the badly deteriorated sewage system, the houses in imminent danger of collapse, the overcrowding, the proliferation of vectors [disease carrying animals], the lack of insecticides and disinfectants, drugstores without the most basic medications, inadequate nourishment—a domestic economy that destroys the psyche of the Cuban People."

hard to find. As a result of these shortages, Cuba's doctors have had to resort to prescribing herbal remedies instead of traditional medicines and using non-Western medical techniques such as acupuncture when anesthetics are not available. Consumer health writer Barbara Jamison explains:

When the United States embargo tightened up soon after Cuba lost the former Soviet Union as a trade partner in the early 1990s, the island was set adrift. U.S.-made medicines and equipment stopped coming into the country, and the economy went into a tailspin. The Cuban Ministry of Health had no choice but to look for less expensive medical alternatives.[53]

In the late 1990s and the early twenty-first century, Cuba's medical community has worked hard to integrate alternative medicine with standard Western techniques. The government encourages people to trust medical approaches, such as acupuncture, that are cheaper but unorthodox. Children learn at school about alternative medicines and are encouraged to grow their own aloe and chamomile for use as medicines. The application of alternative medicine in Cuba is now widespread. As Jamison observes,

Throughout this island country of 11.5 million inhabitants, whether you have to be rushed to a hospital emergency room or are simply visiting your neighborhood clinic for a checkup, you're likely to be treated with a blend of traditional and alternative medicine. Virtually every medical facility on the island has an adjunct alternative clinic, including pharmacies that dispense medicine based on herbal remedies. In the Hospital Ortopidico in Havana, a large teaching institution, you'll notice alongside conventional medical wards entire wings in which patients receive the latest in mud therapy, massage, and acupuncture for osteoporosis, arthritis, and other degenerative diseases.[54]

Some medicines are available in Cuba, but only at special dollar pharmacies, where only foreigners and Communist Party members may shop. Catherine Moses recalls seeing a pharmacist who refused the money of a Cuban woman wishing to buy asthma medicine for her daughters:

[An Angolan diplomat standing in line] asked what was wrong, because he knew the woman had the dollars to pay. The woman was Cuban, and therefore, was not allowed to purchase the medicine for her daughters. The Angolan bought the medicine for her, he said, "Because I am a Christian." For those who have no dollars, there are only two choices: doing without or buying on the black market.[55]

Rumors also prevail that in order to *resolve* their own problems, some physicians who are able to obtain pharmaceuticals will sell them on the black market. If true, this only adds to the shortages faced by ordinary Cubans.

Although Cuba produces a surplus of doctors, ordinary Cubans complain that even getting a doctor's attention has become more difficult. Says Cuban-born "Flora" after a recent trip to Cuba to visit relatives:

Sometimes, people have to be in critical condition or they won't even get looked at by the doctors. And though they may take care of your medical problems, "food-wise" you have problems. If you want food when you're in some hospitals, you have to bring your own, or your relatives have to bring it to you.[56]

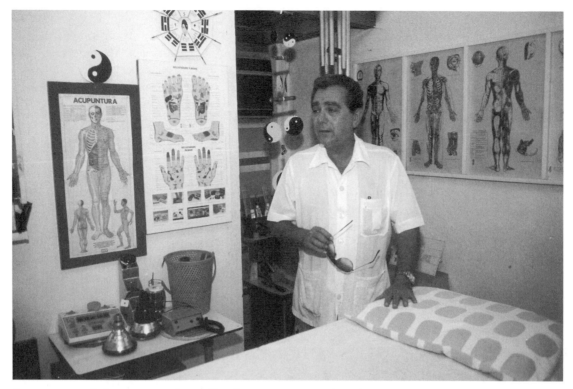

Practitioners of alternative medicine like this acupuncturist have benefited from Cuba's growing shortage of doctors and medical supplies.

Others complain that many Cuban hospitals require patients to provide their own drinking water, sheets, towels, and toiletries.

The departure of doctors and other personnel from medicine for more lucrative jobs in Cuba's changing economy partly explains why doctors are not always available. But the state also requires many doctors to provide medical services for foreigners, even if it means shortchanging their Cuban patients.

Medical Tourism

No longer is Cuba's socialized medicine a not-for-profit enterprise. Instead, the state sells medical services to foreigners willing to go to Cuba for treatment. Government officials say that medical tourism generates up to $20 million to state coffers and helps to offset funding shortages that affect all Cubans. According to Cubanacan Tourism and Health, the state agency in charge of Cuba's medical tourism, about thirty-five hundred tourists visited Cuba in 2002. Attracted by Cuba's reputation for good medical care at cheap prices (as much as 33 percent cheaper than those in the United States), many patients combine a visit to the hospital with a vacation.

Though Cuba's venture in medical tourism is bringing much needed foreign cash into the country, it may be doing so at the expense of the Cuban people. Critics charge that the Cuban government has now created a two-tier medical system that is undermining its socialistic goal. Explains medical writer Miquel A. Faria Jr., MD, "In contrast to the deplorable state of medical services provided to ordinary Cubans, there exists in Cuba special hospitals and clinics with the latest medical technology that cater to two types of patients—foreign tourists with hard cash and the privileged . . . class of the communist [leaders]."[57]

Among the most outspoken critics of Cuba's new policy is Dr. Hilda Molina, the former director of the International Center for Neurological Restoration in Cuba. Among other things, she charges that in its haste to raise money the government engages in unethical practices. She writes:

It is common for Cuban hospitals to advertise services that they do not have the resources to perform. Moreover, they are incapable of guaranteeing results superior to what patients might expect in their own countries. As a result, patients are often inadequately or falsely informed about their condition and steered toward services they may not need.[58]

Many critics of medical tourism, including Cuban doctors, also claim that funds generated by providing medical services for foreigners all too often end up in the hands of Cuba's ruling elite rather than helping fund public programs. According to author

A young girl stands at a Havana pharmacy counter. In times of shortage, medicine is only available to foreigners and Communist Party members.

Dr. Hilda Molina, a prominent Cuban physician, condemns Cuba's practice of selling medical services to foreigners.

Isadora Tattlin, "Foreigners pay in the foreigners' clinics, but the doctors who work there don't get any of it; the doctors still get their same three hundred pesos a month (about eleven dollars) no matter where they work."[59]

Unfazed by the criticism, the Cuban government expects that with the help of tourist agencies, the number of foreign patients to its hospitals will increase 20 percent a year. At the same time, health-care services for the majority of Cubans could be losing ground.

Seeking an Escape in Leisure Time

Although many Cubans spend much of their waking hours foraging and trying to make ends meet, they also find a respite from their hardships during their leisure time. And even though ever watchful government agents are always lurking nearby, Cubans celebrate life in a colorful, richly Caribbean way.

Hanging Out, Cuban Style

A convivial and garrulous people, Cubans, as a rule, enjoy socializing, eating, and drinking with one another. Many simply like to hang out with friends, neighbors, family members, and even strangers on sidewalks, in parks, and at street festivals. Cubans are quick to entertain guests with impromptu parties, even if they cannot always afford to provide enough food and drinks for their guests. Much of what they do for entertainment at these gatherings is talk. Researcher Mona Rosendahl observes:

Conversation is . . . an important part of . . . validating oneself as a true Cuban. In a group of people, the conversations are often about daily events and mutual acquaintances, activities such as weddings, or, of course, what there is to buy where. Being able to tell jokes and being amusing are also important parts of being a full social person. Being quiet is seen as somewhat threatening, and people who

say little are urged to talk and asked what is wrong and why they do not say anything."[60]

Cubans fondness for conversation at parties is evident in the custom of providing special desserts and drinks for *sobre-mesa* (after-dinner) conversations.

Although Cubans spend a lot of time conversing, their talk is often guarded concerning political matters, because they are fearful of saying the wrong thing about the regime and being reported to authorities. They are seldom shy, however, about having lively debates on other topics. Sometimes, they gather in public places for a boisterous exchange of views. One of the most popular of these places is the "Hot Corner" in Havana, where people assemble to argue about the latest news in sports, especially baseball. Often they argue with every resource they have. "Arguing is done not just with words but with the entire body—hands, arms, facial expressions, mock anger. It was more like a dance, a performance,"[61] writes Tony Mendoza.

Cubans have also made an art form of playing with words to tease and entertain others. As travel author Kirsten Ellis explains:

Cubans love bantering jokes, ripostes [quick, sharp replies] and a version of anecdotal word-play, they call "double-morals." In the world of double-morals, nothing is quite as it seems, and every statement or remark can conceal at least one other meaning. Once you have taken this in your stride, you can enjoy the way Cubans have made flirting with contradictions and ambiguities [uncertainties] part of their national character along with a uniquely spirited humor that so often triumphs over adversity. . . . After all, in a country where the national slogan is "Socialismo o Muerte" ("Socialism, or Death"), it could be argued that survival would be impossible without a sense of the absurd, or at the very least, a talent for living in the moment. Like the music and the dancing these semi-secret jokes make the daily weight of life much easier to bear.[62]

Jokes with a double meaning could perhaps poke fun at a Cuban government official who publicly pledges undying allegiance to the revolution but is stealthily stealing from the state coffers to enrich himself.

During the evening, in addition to lively conversations, Cubans find diversion in games of chess, cards, or dominoes. "And when there is light and power, they visit at a neighbor's house to watch government-run television,"[63] says one former resident of Cuba. However, because there are only three government-controlled television stations, Cuban viewers have a limited number of programs to choose from. As a nation, they love soap operas, especially Brazilian-made *telenovelas*,

A group of men discuss baseball in Havana's "Hot Corner," a favorite place for locals to gather and talk about sports.

dubbed in Spanish. Cuban American Tony Mendoza recalls the captivating impact one of these programs had on Cubans during a visit to his homeland:

> The really popular program followed the news: *Women of Sand*, a Brazilian soap. Walking down the streets of Havana between 9:00 P.M. and 10:00 P.M. is a very eerie experience. There is no one on the streets. In every window one can see a blue pulsating glow, the light from the televisions. What's wonderfully surreal is that all the windows are pulsating identically, as if the city were one living organism; everyone is tuned in to *Women of Sand*. The plot revolves around two upper-class women who are identical twins—a very good one and very bad one . . . [who] impersonates the good one and makes a mess of things. A typical soap, without any socialist redeeming values.[64]

Many Cubans also enjoy programs that feature stories about poor people who through luck or hard work improve their lives and obtain higher positions and wealth. Though these ideas are at odds with the Socialist message promoted by Cuban authorities, the state views the programs as harmless entertainment. Other favorites include Cuban-made television programs that carry social messages, such as concern for the environment, and those that portray characters who are confronted with everyday problems, such as life in decrepit housing and the struggle to make ends meet, that resemble those of the viewers themselves.

During daylight hours, when they have time off, Cubans take part in a wide variety of physical activities. Many love to go to the beach or a river. There they stand in chest-deep water, drinking their favorite beverage

and socializing with friends. A few who are lucky enough to have extra money and time engage in personal fitness sports, such as bicycling, jogging, golf, horseback riding, swimming, fishing, and scuba diving. Some even go spelunking in Cuba's vast network of caves and underground passages. Many more Cubans, however, spend much of their leisure time focusing on organized sports.

Love of Sports

Cuba is a sports superpower whose achievements are disproportionate to the country's small size. The government actively encourages Cubans to take part in sports. In fact, in 1961 Castro passed a law giving all citizens the right to participate in sports. As a result, many Cubans love to both watch and play organized sports during their off-duty hours. Among their favorites is jai alai, a sport that originated in the Basque region of Spain. Jai alai players use scoop-shaped racquets to hurl a ball at tremendous speeds in arenas with high-backed walls. Cubans also enjoy wrestling, track-and-field events, volleyball, and fencing. Boxing is especially popular. Almost every school has a boxing ring where boys learn the sport when they are quite young. This interest continues over a lifetime for many Cubans, and Cuba's prowess in boxing has also become a source of national pride. Half of the country's Olympic medals, in fact, have come from boxing. Since 1972 Cuba has won twenty-seven Olympic gold medals.

As popular as boxing is, it barely registers in the national consciousness when compared with the national favorite, *pelota* (baseball). Baseball is Cuba's sports passion. The country is dotted with baseball fields and small stadiums. People of all ages play the game. Instead of soccer, the favorite ball game in neighbor-

A Cuban player slides into second base during a 2003 World Cup game. Baseball is Cuba's number-one spectator sport.

ing Caribbean countries, Cuban children play baseball in alleys or empty lots or wherever they can find space. If they do not have the proper equipment, they play a version of *pelota* known as stickball, in which they use a stick for a bat and catch the ball bare-handed.

Baseball is also the nation's number-one spectator sport. Cubans faithfully follow the baseball season, which runs from mid-November to March. During this time, fans succumb to a kind of national baseball fever and flock to nearby stadiums or keep up with their favorite players and teams on radio and television.

Cubans' passion and skill at baseball is reflected in the many gold medals won by its national team at the Olympic Games. Despite their obvious talent, Cuba's baseball players have little hope of benefiting monetarily. Because Castro outlawed professional sports in the country in 1962, even Cuba's top baseball players earn only about four hundred Cuban pesos a month. Frustrated by the low pay, many ballplayers defect to the United States, where they can earn much bigger sums playing the sport they love. Sometimes, however, the Cuban government ignores its own rules against playing for profit. Although professional sports are illegal in Cuba, many members of the nation's women's volleyball team—one of the best in the world—play professionally in Italy during part of the year, though most of their earnings are turned over to the Cuban government.

Tough Times for Cuba's Runners

Marathon runner and writer for the *Colorado Daily* newspaper, Mike Sandrock, gives this account in *Footnotes*, the online magazine for the Road Runners Club of America, of his encounter with poorly equipped Cuban runners during a recent trip to Cuba.

"One runner I became friends with was Eglis Delis Roca. She was a top 400-meter hurdler several years ago, clocking 59 seconds. After having her son, she didn't run for six years. Now, at 28, she has resumed training for the 2,000-meter steeplechase and marathon. I was shocked when I first met her at the track. She was training in mismatched canvas shoes, different colors and different sizes, along with a ragged T-shirt and frayed cotton shorts. She doesn't own a pair of socks. She lives in a house across from the Moncada army barracks, where the revolution started on July 26, 1953. (Fidel Castro was captured after the attack, and the front entrance is still riddled with bullet holes.)

Eglis, her husband, and her child share one room in an old colonial-era house. Hanging on the wall, which looks like it hasn't been painted since the triumph of the revolution, are the numerous medals she won as a hurdler.

Every day, Eglis wears the same cotton shorts and T-shirt, similar to what we wore in gym classes a generation ago. But Eglis's equipment woes aren't unique. Many of the young Cuban runners train in shoes that should be in the trash. The shoes are made in Cuba or China, look something like Keds, and cost about 100 pesos, or $5. . . .

There are two problems with that. First, because of the blockade, there are few decent running shoes to be found. Second, while there are some 'dollar stores' selling Reebok shoes, they are the same price as those in the United States, which means there is no way an athlete could afford them. So the runners improvise, reusing the upper parts of their spikes and shoes, replacing the bottoms with cheap rubber that cracks and falls apart after a few weeks. In Cuba, the special period is the mother of invention.

The top athletes have it better. At the sports city, about 50 national team athletes live in dormitories attached to the track. . . . Before the collapse of the Soviet Union, it was not legal to own dollars, and teachers, coaches, and doctors were among the best-paid people in society. Now, with dollars the currency needed to buy even the most basic items, such as shampoo, clothes, and meat, it is bartenders and others in the tourist trade who have replaced professionals as the envied people in society."

The low pay it grants players notwithstanding, the Cuban government takes pride in the nation's athletic prowess and goes to great lengths to identify promising athletes and train them at one of the country's fifteen special sports schools. There students receive basic schooling, but they also receive state-sponsored athletic training to prepare them for international competition. Later, if they become accomplished in their respective sports, the athletes receive extra benefits from the state, such as the right to live in elegant villas for life. According to Angel Iglesias, vice president of the Cuban National Institute of Sport, Physical Education, and Recreation:

We had athletes before the revolution. But we didn't have sport. We didn't have a coherent system to develop talent, to help any athlete from anywhere in Cuba reach his full potential. Now we do. This hasn't come cheaply. It's cost us. But it's worth it, because our youth is involved in sport here, and not in drugs or violence. It's one of the triumphs of the revolution.[65]

As is true throughout society, Cuba's sports enthusiasts face hardships. For example, a scarcity of funds makes it hard for Cuban athletes to get the uniforms, equipment, and training that they desperately need. Says Adelberto Cuvas, a Cuban national marathon coach, "It's not easy for our runners. Sometimes they don't have good food to eat, and the hemoglobin levels in the blood are low.

Athletes in the U.S. can be in good form because they have more to eat. Not here."[66]

Festivals and Holidays

Even though most Cubans must struggle every day to make ends meet, they do find time to celebrate numerous public holidays and festivals. On May 1, for example, throngs of Cubans fill the streets with parades to honor the workers of their country.

The biggest and most popular festival is Carnival, which is celebrated in July to commemorate the Cuban revolution. It is a noisy, exuberant festival of food, drink, music, and dance. Dancers wear elaborate costumes and dance the Congo de Santiago and other dances, as musicians beat pulsating rhythms on wide, thin African drums.

Young girls adjust their headdresses before the start of the annual Carnival parade. The Cuban Carnival commemorates the events of the 1959 revolution.

The Cuban government supports and promotes most of these events, especially those that attract foreign tourists. Other events may be disregarded or even denounced by Castro's regime. Some events face funding problems depending on the country's economic woes; still others are the targets of Castro's censors and face the threat of being closed down. For instance, for a long time the government has denounced and discouraged La Fiesta del Quince—a day celebrated by a family when a teenage girl reaches her fifteenth birthday and is formally considered to have become a woman. For those Cubans who can afford it, a *quince* is a once-in-a-lifetime ballroom affair, in which fifteen young couples—one representing each year of the young girl's life—take part in the festivities by dancing Cuban casino dances of the 1930s and 1940s. Girls wear formal gowns and their escorts don suits. At the end of the evening, which is filled with dancing and feasting, someone toasts the young woman being honored and then her friends present her with fifteen candles, each of which represents a year of her life.

Fewer and fewer Cuban girls are celebrating a *quince*, however. Critics suspect that Castro's government opposes the festival because it hopes to weaken Cubans' ties to tradition and replace them with new ties to Castro's government instead. In addition, given Cuba's present economic difficulties, few families can afford to host such a gala event.

Castro's regime has also taken a similar stance toward certain religious holidays. For decades, the state had banned the celebration of Christmas and Easter, presumably in an attempt to weaken the power of the Catholic Church. In recent years, however, the state has allowed these celebrations to return.

The Performing Arts

The Cuban government is an avid supporter of the performing arts—as long as performances do not undermine Castro's authority. However, the state has tolerated mild criticism of life in Cuba expressed in many recent theater dramas. One of them is the play *The Other Tempest*, a reworking of a play written by sixteenth-century English playwright William Shakespeare. According to Andrew Cawthorne, a writer for the Reuters news agency, "The [play's] main character, Prospero, and the larger-than-life figure of Cuba's President Castro are none too subtle. The Italian duke is portrayed as a hot-tempered bearded man who is seeking to build Utopia [a perfect society] on a distant tropical island but is denounced as a tyrant by his critics."[67]

Another new popular play is *The Ideal Place*, a comedy about Cuba's new tourist industry and the shortages that trouble Cubans. At one point in the play, a magician donates the rabbit he pulls out of a hat for his magic shows to his hungry family for a meal. "The play avoids direct swipes at Cuba's Communist leaders but documents hilariously, and poignantly, the daily economic struggle of ordinary people and the second-class citizenship they sometimes feel at seeing the privileges tourists enjoy,"[68] Cawthorne explains.

Castro supporters claim that these plays and others like them prove that Castro tolerates free expression. Critics, however, point out that the government merely allows such expression because the plays are performed before relatively small groups and therefore present no real threat to those in power. Cawthorne adds that some observers also point out that the theater serves as "a safety valve for Cuba's intellectual and artistic community, permitting sufficient space to keep

Cuban Rhythm

In his essay "Making Music," which appears in *Cuba: True Stories*, edited by Tom Miller, English travel writer Henry Shukman explains how the streets of the town of Boracoa in the Oriente region of Cuba are transported into a street party when the sun sets.

"As darkness falls, makeshift barbecues appear on the streets, salsa tapes start to play, and fashions from every decade of the century emerge—evening dresses with slits to here, nip-waisted little '40s numbers, Audrey Hepburn suits, skin-tight tiger-striped flares a la Mick Jagger circa '72 and hemless micros. . . . Meanwhile, musicians arrive on bicycles, carrying instruments on their backs and in the space of fifteen minutes—as long as it takes night to fall—the town turns into a music buffet.

First there's the brass band under the laurel trees of the Parque Central [Central Park], screeching and honking its way through "El Bodequero," the ancient horns buttressed by a bank of African percussion. Then the rumba gets going into the colonnade outside the *casa de cultural* [House of Culture], led by a team of five drummers and singers and two mesmeric [spell-binding] dancers whose feet perform miracles of high-speed intricacy. But the most sought-after action, once you have pushed through the throngs of black mini-dressed *senoritas* dancing to street sound systems, is in the *casa de la trova*.

Every Cuban town has one of these, a kind of village hall cum concert hall with a busy rum bar. On a little stage adorned with rudimentary murals, before several rows of dutiful listeners, the town troubadours vaunt their wares. Soneros of all ages, from teens to teetering, test their ability to rouse a crowd. A backing band of bass, guitar, and shaker-scraper-bangers, grinning and dancing in formation, provide a springboard to launch the maestros [master performers].

As night wears on . . . the rows of chairs are abandoned in favor of dancing that would shame any Miami salsa slicker. . . . This is a night without end, the kind Cubans live for."

them from becoming frustrated but not enough to threaten the system."[69]

Because the state sponsors many of Cuba's performing arts and other entertainment, Cubans from all walks of life are able to attend films, concerts, ballets, and other artistic performances at a fraction of the cost charged for such events in many other countries. Tickets often cost only the equivalent of five to twenty-five U.S. cents.

These performances range from those that showcase Cuba's folkloric traditions to high culture events, such as the International Ballet Festival. Havana hosts international events such as the Havana Jazz Festival, the International Lyric Festival, the Guitar Festival, and the International Festival of New Latin-American Cinema.

City dwellers can enjoy traditional Cuban music and dance at a *casa del trova*—an entertainment center that is a cross between a bar, a dance hall, and a concert hall. They can sample other forms of culture, including movies and art exhibits, at a *casa de la cultura*. In big cities such as Havana, people can view plays or attend concerts performed by the National Symphony Orchestra and other world-class musical groups. Cuba's renowned National Ballet also makes tours of Cuban cities when it is not performing abroad.

Although these big city events are not readily accessible to all Cubans, most towns have a theater and a movie house. They also have cabarets that showcase nightly performances by singers, musicians, magicians, and other performers.

Music Lovers

No matter where they are, most Cubans respond quickly to the sound of music. If none is available, they make their own on the spot. Music reaches deep into Cuban culture and personal identity. As an anonymous Cuban writer puts it, "Cubans are musical when they walk, talk, move, even look; with music they go to war. A house without a radio blaring day and night is unthinkable. Cubans chat-up with music and at times are even conceived to music. Cubans sing and clap from the cradle to the grave, from their children in the cots to their burial set to the sound of a favorite tune."[70]

Although Cubans of all ages enjoy music from the United States and Europe, such as hip-hop, jazz, rap, and hard rock, they also have a special fondness for their own home-grown Cuban music. This unique genre has its roots in the musical traditions of many cul-

Music is an integral part of Cuban culture, and most Cubans have a great passion for dancing.

tures. Flamenco-style guitar playing and ballads are mixed with melodies from Italy and France. Cuban music also contains influences from the now-vanished indigenous people of Cuba and the drumming and singing of the Congolese and Yoruba of West Africa, introduced to Cuba in the days of slavery. In fact, many Cuban performers still sing in the Yoruban language rather than in Spanish. "Overall, it is accurate to say that Cuban music often fuses African sources and aspects of Santeria [an African-rooted religion] rhythms with traditional folk dance music along with jazz, rock, and classical elements,"[71] writes Kirsten Ellis.

Cuban music comes in many varieties; one of the most popular is a form called *son*. Its distinctive beat is produced with two heavy sticks, improvised lyrics, and a frequently repeated chorus. *Son-charanga* and *son-cangue* are variants of *son* music that are heard across the island.

Many Cuban musicians also love to play at *descargas* (jam sessions), which pop up almost spontaneously. Some of these feature Cuban jazz, which is popular not only in Cuba but also around the world. The stature of Cuban jazz is a far cry from what it once was. In the early days of the revolution, the state discouraged Cubans from playing jazz music, because it was closely associated with the land of its birth—the hated United States. But in recent years, the government has backed off, and jazz has flourished. American guitarist Ry Cooder recorded the music of well-known aging Cuban jazz artists and popularized it in the West. The U.S. government has taken steps to prevent Cooder from continuing his project, fining him one hundred thousand dollars under the Trading with the Enemy Act—part of a collection of American laws aimed at hurting trade with Cuba.

Love of Dance

Most Cubans are not content to merely listen to music; they are also quick to leap to their feet and dance, no matter where they are. Foreigners are sometimes shocked at the energy and sensuality exhibited by Cuban dancers. Cubans, as a rule, are very physical dancers. Among their favorite dances is the rumba—a type of ballroom dancing with Afro-Cuban folk origins. Typically, rumba dancers stand cheek to cheek and make distinctive, sensual, side-to-side hip movements. Cubans love rumba so much that a couple dancing in a tavern might be accompanied by spectators beating on pots and bottles with spoons.

Other dances that Cubans enjoy are a slow dance called a *yambus* and the Columbia, which is performed by men with knives and machetes. However, the dance dearest to the hearts of many Cubans by far is the tango, a sensual form of ballroom dancing. As an elderly Cuban musician explained to British TV reporter Stephen Smith, "It's poetry, it's kindness, it's tragedy. It is the Bible of life."[72]

Appreciating Art

Although the arts generally bring pleasure, appreciation, and enlightenment to human beings, totalitarian governments are wary of them because they also are vehicles for communicating dissent. Cuban officials therefore sometimes censor art and punish artists whose works violate what the government deems acceptable. On the other hand, since the early days of the revolution the state has encouraged art as long as it conforms to Communist Party guidelines. As Castro once put it, "With the Revolution, everything. Against the Revolution nothing."[73]

A poster commemorating the forty-fifth anniversary of the Cuban revolution hangs above a Havana road. Such commemorative art is quite common throughout Cuba.

Unidos luchamos...
45 Unidos vencemos
Aniversario del Triunfo de la Revolución

Even though such censorship imparts a chilling effect on many Cuban artists, they still produce an astonishing display of work seen in museums and galleries across the country. If some artists resent government monitoring of their work, others embrace revolutionary themes and feature them in their work. Many such works appear in the form of poster art—a distinctly Cuban mode of expression that usually depicts revolutionary themes or those that advance the ideals of socialism. Mural-sized posters can be found in the cities, and billboards along the highways commemorate revolutionary events and revolutionary heroes such as Che Guevara.

Many Cubans also spend their leisure time appreciating Cuba's wide assortment of folk art. Among their favorite works are those inspired by Afro-Cuban religions, which express spiritual devotion to various deities in beadwork, garments, cloth panels, metalwork, wood carvings, altars, musical instruments, paintings, and other art forms.

The Oppressive Shadow of Government

Despite the government's overt support for artistic expression, many Cuban artists, whether in the fine arts, performing arts, or dramatic arts, feel stifled by the state. Now and then, depending on the political mood, the government pressures musicians, performers, writers, and artists to conform to the state's idea of what is permissible. Cuban authorities can show their displeasure in many ways. They can deny musical groups permission to play at certain venues or forbid artists to exhibit certain paintings. Sometimes their decisions appear arbitrary. For instance, during her recent residence in Cuba, author Isadora Tattlin learned that a government official had decreed that artists could no longer paint nudes, pictures of Fidel Castro, or symbols of national sovereignty.

The state may act in a discreet way to stop a performance. For instance, it may cut off electricity to a band that is having an illegal rehearsal. Or Castro's agents may act boldly and seize a novelist's manuscript that is thought to be too subversive. Even worse punishment might result for those who drift too far away from what the state considers acceptable. Such government control does great damage to many people. For one thing, it frustrates artistic expression and causes unhappiness among the nation's creative individuals. It also deprives other Cubans of various ways of experiencing art and entertainment. Finally, it stymies another important function of art, one that implores others, including government officials, to critically examine their own society and attempt to improve it.

Cuba's creative community struggles to *resolve* this problem in many ways. Some artists give in to government pressure and try to remain within the confines set up by the government. Others flee Cuba to have their works published or exhibited abroad, even if it means facing repercussions at home. A few work in secrecy and abandon their dreams of presenting their work to fellow Cubans.

Buoying the Cuban Spirit

Even before the Communist takeover, many Cubans had long harbored resentment against the Catholic Church, whose hierarchy had supported Spain when the Cuban people were fighting for independence. When the Spanish finally departed the island, Cuban authorities rebuked the church by passing laws that clearly separated church and state. As a result, the church lost much of its influence on the hearts and souls of the Cuban people.

A general disinterest in Catholicism was replaced by outright hostility when Castro came to power. Though Castro never went so far as to ban religion, he made life unpleasant for believers. From the start of the revolution, he proclaimed that Cuba's new government was atheistic and accused religious organizations of offering false hope and empty promises to the Cuban people. Despite the fact that the Cuban constitution protects individual freedom of religion, the state has persecuted and oppressed religious leaders and believers during the past four and a half decades. During this time, the government also seized and nationalized church lands. In addition, the Communist Party denied membership to anyone who expressed religious beliefs. From 1965 to 1967 Cuba's Communists also rounded up various priests, ministers, and others who made religion a way of life and imprisoned them in forced labor camps, along with others whom Castro's regime considered social scum. For the next thirty years these religious figures continued

to live in the shadow of a government intolerant of religion.

The state even carried its antireligious campaign to the classroom, closing all Catholic schools permanently. At various times Castro's agents persecuted religious students. School officials and teachers, for instance, were required to publicly humiliate students caught wearing crosses or bringing Bibles to school. In addition, students who openly professed their religious beliefs were denied entrance into Cuba's institutions of higher learning.

A Change in Government Policy

The Cuban government has softened its hostility to religion in recent years. The first step in this direction came in 1991, when Communist officials abolished the ban on membership in the party by religious believers. A year later the state declared Cuba was no longer an atheistic state. In 1998 the government allowed Pope John Paul II to visit Cuba, making him the first pope ever to visit the country since the Communists took power.

Castro did not explain his apparent change of heart. Some observers suspect that the dictator realized the importance of appearing friendlier toward religion to polish Cuba's tarnished human rights image abroad. According to this school of thought, Castro needs to curry favor with other countries to obtain foreign aid and trade agreements to aid Cuba's ailing economy, and softening his government's image furthers that goal. Some observers think he may also recognize the fact that growing numbers of Cubans have turned to religion to help buoy their spirits during hard times. To persecute them harshly would surely generate condemnation from other nations and hamper efforts to establish closer ties with potential donor nations.

Castro may have another motive in mind. The nation's dictator may also hope to enlist organized religion in an effort to enhance his own popularity, which has declined during the nation's tough economic times. Writes journalist John W. Kennedy for *Christianity Today*:

After nearly four decades of unrealized communist dreams, Cubans are ripe for change. There is a spiritual hunger in the land, a void that Marxism has been unable to fill. Out of a population of 11 million, the number of active Christians is approaching 1 million, the most ever. Castro realizes Christians now represent a potent force. He met with 70 representatives from 31 denominations, primarily members of the Cuban Council of Churches, in a nine-hour meeting on

Castro welcomes Pope John Paul II to Cuba in 1998. Critics accuse Castro of orchestrating the pope's visit to improve the country's tarnished human rights image.

November 24 [1998]. Castro asked the religious leaders to pray for the nation's economic problems, including decreased sugar production, declining foreign investments, and a dearth of international credit. The dictator is willing to bend in order to preserve his revolution—and his power.[74]

A Christian Revival

In the wake of these changes, the presence of religion in the daily lives of Cubans has grown stronger. Nowhere is this better seen than in the country's dominant religion, Catholicism. Since the pope's visit, the number of Cubans professing to be Catholic has steadily risen. Many older Cubans are returning to the church, saying they are trying to rediscover their religious roots. For others the church has become a refuge from the depressing realities of everyday life. The church is also opening its doors to many young people who have become disillusioned with the revolution and have turned to Catholicism to find meaning and direction to their lives. Catherine Moses observes:

The Catholic church is more for Cubans than a religious institution. Today it is an

A woman (right) receives blessings from a priest. Since the pope's 1998 visit, Cuba has experienced a resurging interest in Catholicism.

educator, a social worker, and a harbor from the madness of life. Young people are coming to the Catholic church today not only to find something to believe in and a direction in their lives but also to find a sense of history. They have known nothing but Revolution. While they might be well informed about Soviet history, their knowledge of their own nation's past consists of only what the Revolution found convenient to tell them. The Catholic church has taken on this daunting task of teaching history.[75]

Although the church imparts knowledge to young people concerning their heritage, it still cannot open academic schools. However, it does serve as a source for some medicine and caregiving services for members of the congregation who are ill. The church also provides after-school programs for children.

Because the church lacks complete independence from the government and is always vulnerable to the whim of Castro, it does not play a leading role in opposing state repression in Cuba. Nonetheless, some Cubans believe it functions as the conscience of the island, because many priests and bishops publicly speak out about many of the social and economic problems facing the country. A statement issued from the Conference of Catholic Bishops addressed some of these concerns:

> What has happened in Cuba? The economic crisis is quite evident, and . . . many want to find a quick way to improve the conditions of their lives. But there is something more worrisome . . . which is not political. . . . The fundamental equality of all men and women . . . based on the intrinsic dignity of the human being, created by God in his image, is not the same

as the . . . [government's policy of creating equality by placing] in the same category, as far as type of work, vacation, and salary, the doctor who saves the life of a patient in open heart surgery as the machine operator in a textile mill.[76]

As the Catholic Church struggles to reassert its importance in everyday Cuban life, Protestantism also shows signs of modest growth in Cuba, though its number of adherents is far fewer than the number of Catholics. Today only about 4 percent of Cubans are practicing Protestants. Among the almost fifty Protestant denominations represented in Cuba, the most common are the Baptist and Pentecostal churches.

Cuba's Minority Religion Makes a Comeback

Judaism is also making a comeback in Cuba. Before the revolution nearly fifteen thousand Jews called Cuba home. Many European Jews had settled in Cuba at the end of World War II, but when Castro's forces took over Cuba, many Jewish residents, who had suffered terrible persecution by German Nazis, feared yet more oppression and departed for Israel, the United States, and other lands. During the following decades, only a fraction of the original Jewish population remained in Cuba. Although the government did not unleash anti-Semitic purges that the exiles had feared, Jews who remained in Cuba did face severe problems. Like everyone else, they endured daily hardships in the wake of the Soviet collapse. In addition, disruptions in food production made it hard for observant Jews to maintain a kosher diet—consisting of food prepared to rules established by Jewish scholars. Hungry Jewish Cubans were even forced to eat forbidden foods, such as pork and shellfish, which are considered unclean and unfit for consumption.

Life, however, has improved for Cuban Jews in recent years. Castro's softening stance on religious observance, combined with an influx of financial aid from foreign Jewish organizations, has helped Cuban Jews rebuild their communities. "We are OK here. There is no anti-Semitism. We used to be isolated, but things have changed,"[77] Dr. Jose Miller, a retired surgeon and a leader in the Cuban Jewish community, recently told American journalist Dan Freedman.

Meanwhile, as Christianity and Judaism make a comeback, another religion, Santeria, continues to grow in Cuba. Once considered a cult, it is now so widespread that many consider it Cuba's real religion.

Santeria

Santeria is a fusion of Catholicism and elements of the Lucumi religion practiced by the Yoruba tribe in West Africa. It emerged in Cuba during the nineteenth century among slaves who tried to preserve the religious practices of their African ancestors. Historians believe that when slave masters banned all African religions in Cuba, their slaves responded by pretending to revere Catholic saints instead. However, they were really using the saints to represent divine beings, or

Santeria Fests

An estimated 70 percent of the Cuban population practices some aspect of the Afro-Cuban religion Santeria. In this passage from his book *Afro-Cuban Religions*, Miquel Barnet, director of the Fernando Ortiz Foundation in Havana, provides a description of some of the religion's celebrations.

"There are a number of religious fests and ceremonies in Santeria. The most striking are those dedicated to a particular saint. During these ceremonies, one can express feelings of joy and thankfulness to specific saints and feelings of dissatisfaction or disapproval toward others. . . .

There are also celebrations attended by large numbers of people. Anyone can participate, and the purpose is simply fun and entertainment. . . . During these secular celebrations, *bata* drums may not be played and *guiros* or *abwes*—musical instruments made from gourds—are used instead. These

are always accompanied by an iron instrument shaped like a bell without a clapper, called *agogo*, or else by the metal part of a hoe.

These bata drums are played during the sacred initiation ceremonies or ceremonies for the saints' birthdays: the *iya* or mother, which is the biggest; the medium-sized *itotele;* and the *okonkolo*, which is the smallest one and has the highest tone. These drums are given food offerings because each one contains a numen or semigod which has a magical secret, *ana*, which may not be revealed by those who construct and play them.

At sunset the exhausting beat of the bata comes to an end. The drums are taken back to the sacred room (*igbodu*) and remain there until the next ceremony, which always takes place during the hours of daylight. Afterwards *abwes* are played, and with no time restrictions, the sacred or semiprofane celebrations can continue until after midnight."

orishas, of their own Lucumi religion. Eventually, the Spanish word for saints (*santos*) gave rise to the word *Santeria*, or Way of the Saints.

Today Santeria is flourishing in Cuba. Practitioners of the religion believe in one supreme god and the existence of hundreds of orishas; however, most followers focus on only about twenty orishas that they believe influence their daily lives. To please these spirits and thus avoid bad luck, adherents turn to *babalaos* (high priests), who act as go-betweens with the spiritual world. *Babalaos* offer spiritual guidance and cast spells by using coconut shells and cards in ritualistic ways. Adherents of Santeria believe that during these rituals, the orishas can be coaxed from the spirit world to address the needs of the faithful and help them live better lives. By using certain colors, animals, and drum beats, orishas can also be enticed to mount a Santeria priest, who then begins a symbolic dance with movements that represent the characteristics of a particular orisha. During the ceremonies, orishas allegedly speak through the mouths of the *babalaos*, answering questions and giving advice. In return for these services, followers of Santeria make offerings of plants or food or sacrifices of animals such as goats and chickens.

Traditionally, Santeria has been associated with Cuba's poor and underprivileged classes, particularly those among the country's black population. But today Santeria is practiced throughout Cuban society. One estimate holds that up to 70 percent of the Cuban population observes Santeria in some way. Many practicing Catholics, for instance, dabble with Santeria to ward off sickness and obtain good luck. Performers often invoke Santeria chants in their lyrics and imitate the movements of *babalaos* in their dances.

Some observers think Santeria may have a widespread presence because, unlike Cuba's Christian faiths, it lacks a structured organization with strong national leaders. Castro may thus not have perceived it as a threat to his own power and saw no need to suppress the religion, as he did Christianity. In addition, these observers suggest that in the past Castro tolerated Santeria, hoping it would increase in popularity and thereby weaken the Catholic Church.

Other Religions and Belief Systems

Cuba is home to other Afro-Caribbean religions, such as the Sociedad de Secreta Abakua (Secret Society of Abakua). This mysterious society consists of a network of secret lodges, or chapters, for men only. Among other practices, members take part in hooded masquerades and processions that involve sorcery and punishment and purification rites. Some Cubans also practice voodoo, an import from Haiti, which, like Santeria, mixes elements of nature worship, spells, and spirits with elements of Catholicism, such as the use of chants, prayers, candles, bells, and the sign of the cross.

Spiritualism

As a rule, Cubans do not adhere to just one religion. Instead, they mix various elements of Christianity and Santeria and blend them with aspects of the occult to enrich their spiritual lives. One of the more popular approaches to Cuban mysticism is found in spiritism (spiritualism). Practitioners focus their attention on *más allá* (the supernatural side of life). They use séances, psychic

Santeria, a fusion of Catholicism and the Lucumi religion of the West African Yoruba tribe, is practiced throughout Cuban society. Here, a group of devotees participate in a ceremony.

readings, dreaming of future events, and the conjuring of visions to produce insights into *más allá*. They also hold spiritual masses, which are a combination of Catholic mass and spiritualistic practices.

The Virgin of Charity

Almost all Cubans, no matter what religion or spiritual belief system they practice, have something in common: They revere a patron saint unique to Cuba, La Virgen de Caridad (the Virgin of Charity), who is represented by a legendary statue. Catholics believe the statue is a representative of the Virgin Mary. Practitioners of Santeria also venerate it, though they identify the statue as the deity

Odrun. Even avowed atheists revere the Virgin.

A three-towered church, perched on a hill in the small copper mining town of El Cobre, located twelve miles outside Havana, serves as the shrine for Cuba's most venerated icon. Displayed inside the church is a fifteen-inch wooden statue of the Virgin Mary, dressed in a golden cloak and crown. According to popular belief, in 1606 two men and a ten-year-old boy were in a storm-tossed boat in the Bay of Nipe near Santiago de Cuba when they heard a voice say, "I am the Virgin of Charity." To their astonishment they saw a small wooden effigy of the Virgin Mary floating among the waves on a board. The statue was of a mixed-race—half white, half black—woman holding a Christian cross in one hand

and cradling a mixed-race baby Jesus in her other arm. The statue wore a sign inscribed with the words, "I am the Virgin of Charity."

Following that day, the icon traveled from one place to another and became a holy relic. Finally, a shrine was built to house it in the town of El Cobre. Over the years, many legends have emerged of the various blessings and miracles the Virgin has bestowed upon the Cuban people. For example, it is said that the Virgin helped the descendants of slaves who were being forced to work in copper mines near El Cobre. Her intervention on their behalf led to their release from captivity in 1782.

Today scores of Cubans from all walks of life arrive in El Cobre every day to show their respect to the Virgin and to ask her favors and blessings. To dramatize their devotion, many pious believers crawl or walk on their knees

A Pilgrimage to the Virgin of Charity

The excerpt from Christopher Hunt's book *Waiting for Fidel* describes the devotion he saw Cubans display to the statue of the Virgin of Charity—Cuba's holiest shrine.

"Recessed from three arched entrances, the heavy wooden doors were shut firmly when we reached the top of the drive. Aristide led me to the rear, where a parking lot overlooked the town and the brown gas that copper mining had left on the land. A gang of peddlers sprinted toward a foreigner who might need candles, crosses, or shiny stones. Evasive actions took us out of the heat and into the cool of a hall in the back of the basilica. To the right, a marble staircase led to a chapel.

At the top of the stairs a middle-age woman wearing a wooden cross around her neck held out her hands. She accepted my flowers and added them to the dozens of bouquets left by other worshipers. A sweep of her hand invited me to join the ten Cubans already in the chapel. I watched the pilgrims cross themselves and kiss their fingers before kneeling to pray. Then the men and women looked up, their faces open with the wonder of children listening to Grandpa's stories.

The becalmed gazes were directed toward the glass case holding the Virgin, who could be rotated to face the congregation of the cavernous chamber behind the chapel. Propped on a silver bowl on a marble stand the statue looked like a doll, a doll dressed in a pyramid of a gold robe decorated with the national crest of Cuba. The Virgin also wore a crown, as did the baby in her arms. No amount of finery, however, could make me understand the evident devotion inspired by the wooden statue.

Back downstairs, I understood better. Cubans came to El Cobre bearing objects symbolic of their unfulfilled prayers. Cripples asked for mobility by leaving tiny legs cut from a sheet of metal. Amputees prayed by leaving symbols of arms and hands. Thousands of other dainty cutouts of cars, houses, and anything else a Cuban might want dangled from hooks on the wall above a silver altar. Some pilgrims left clearer signs at the Shrine of Miracles. High on the wall, crutches hung beside a set of leg braces.

But El Cobre wasn't just about requests. Another display showed offerings left by grateful Cubans. Several women gave thanks by leaving braided ponytails. Beside the hair lay a license plate and a guitar. A nurse left her diploma."

up the steep, winding road that leads to the church. There they pray for miracles and the Virgin's blessings and leave small tokens of their gratitude, such as toys, dolls, and jewelry. Some leave more personal gifts: a yellow pencil from a student to express thankfulness for passing exams or a kidney stone to show the results of a successful operation. Says a Cuban American named Angelica who recently revisited Cuba:

> Before the Virgin are the usual dolls dressed as brides, or with street clothes, and household things, like a cup; also jewelry, such as a bracelet, or a ring. There was a particular gift that struck me and made me cry. It was a large poster board (like the ones used for school projects) which said "Mother, don't forget your children who are in prison." That the poster would be allowed to remain was amazing, because most of the people in jail are political prisoners. There was another letter from a mother asking the Virgin for protection for her son making the trip across the Florida straits. Mother-to-mother, that's the way to go![78]

The Virgin is more than a religious icon for the people of Cuba. She is also a symbol that binds the Cuban people. "It's an important icon to the whole nation," says Cuban-

Cubans pray before the statue of the Virgin of Charity in El Cobre, Cuba. The Virgin is Cuba's most revered icon.

born Manuel Caberio. "Castro might destroy a family with the revolution and that would be tolerated by the Cuban people; but he wouldn't dare touch the icon."[79]

The Watchful Eye of Government

Although the Cuban government has eased its restrictions on religious belief, many domestic religious groups continue to be subject to some form of harassment and persecution—particularly those that are not registered with the government. As the U.S. State Department observed in a 2002 report: "The Ministry of Interior still engages in efforts to control and monitor the country's religious institutions, including surveillance, infiltration, and harassment of religious professionals and laypersons."[80] For example, religious congregations that wish to hold outdoor processions or other religious observances must first obtain permission from the government.

Although the law in Cuba allows the building of new churches, government officials seldom grant the permits necessary for construction. Therefore, thousands of Cubans hold religious services in their homes. In fact, growing numbers of adherents of various denominations congregate in residential homes or abandoned houses to worship. The Reverend Pablo Ciedro Ariansa, an evangelical pastor in Havana, says there are several reasons for this growth in "house churches:"

First, there are so many people coming to the churches in Cuba today that there is not room in the existing denominational churches. Second, there are tremendous transportation problems in Cuba. The economic situation is horrible and there are no cars. We can't afford taxis and the local bus system is dysfunctional and all but broken down. Most buses run about two hours late. This all makes it very difficult to attend a church more than 5 km from one's home. Third, house churches are growing very quickly today as a result of these factors, so of course we are happy to accommodate our growing numbers of believers.[81]

This practice, however, is still dangerous. State officials often fine or evict religious people from their homes as punishment for some perceived infraction. According to a religious watchdog group, International Christian Concern (ICC), Cuban authorities have even bulldozed the private residences of some Cubans who used their homes for religious purposes. Castro's government often targets religious groups who are not on the government's officially approved list. The ICC also reports that in 1999 Cuban troops confiscated and burned thousands of Bibles printed in the United States because they were considered subversive.

Despite these acts of government oppression, religious groups in Cuba enjoy much more freedom of action than most other nongovernment organizations. For example, Cubans who gather to discuss political, social, and economic ideas that deviate from communism find themselves targeted for severe forms of harassment and punishment. Those few dissidents who are bold and brave enough to openly oppose Castro and his regime and call for democratic reforms face the full wrath of Castro's government.

Dissidence and Departure

During his many years in power, Fidel Castro has repeatedly demonstrated his willingness to use force, repression, and other means to intimidate Cubans and keep them from opposing his rule. In his eyes, these means are justifiable because they quell opposition to revolutionary forces that Castro says are necessary to create a more just society.

In Cuba, Castro's courts send people to jail for political crimes. These offenses fall into one of three categories. Some actions are considered to be dangerous to the state. Other offenses involve irreverence toward or defiance of authority. The third kind of offense is spreading enemy propaganda. Those convicted of committing any of these offenses can be severely punished. Government officials seldom deny that they take harsh measures against dissidents, saying that they must be tough on enemies of the revolution to preserve the Communist way of life, and to protect Cuba against the United States. On the other hand, critics of such policies insists the state's real goal is to intimidate the populace and preserve Castro's control over the people.

Author and former political prisoner Carlos Alberto Montaner writes that since the start of Castro's rule the dictator was convinced that

> intimidation and fear were important tools in governing. He believed punishment, and learning from the experience of others were two of the best weapons of

power. This is clearly reflected in his personal correspondence, where there are frequent references to Robespierre [a brutal dictator during the French Revolution] and his admiration for revolutionary terror.[82]

Castro is unwaveringly convinced that communism is the destiny of Cuba. Anyone who does not share this vision is in serious trouble with state authorities.

From the early days of his rule, Castro has ruthlessly persecuted and punished those who dare to dissent. Although it does not routinely execute political prisoners as it did in the past, the Cuban government still severely punishes dissenters. Its vast spy system continues to report the names of those who disagree with the government or who wish to reform the system. According to a 2003 report on human rights violations in Cuba prepared by the U.S. State Department's Bureau of Democracy, Human Rights, and Labor:

> Prisoners died in jail due to lack of medical care. Members of the security forces and prison officials continued to beat and abuse detainees and prisoners, including human rights activists. The Government failed to prosecute or sanction adequately members of the security forces and prison guards who committed abuses. Prison conditions remained harsh and life threatening. The authorities routinely continued to harass, threaten, arbitrarily

arrest, detain, imprison, and defame human rights advocates and members of independent professional associations, including journalists, economists, doctors, and lawyers, often with the goal of coercing them into leaving the country.[83]

The U.S. government further charges that Castro uses exile within and outside the country to stifle those who speak out against state abuses. In addition, say U.S. authorities, Cuba denies political dissidents and human rights activists due process of law and fair trials. It also does not allow Cubans to exercise free speech, press, assembly, and association. According to a 2003 report on Cuba by Amnesty International, "[Cuban] authorities continued to try to discourage dissent by harassing suspected critics of the government. Suspected dissidents were subjected to short-term detention, frequent summonses, threats, eviction, loss of employment and restrictions on movement."[84]

A Foreigner Feels the Chill of the CDR

The Committee for the Defense of the Revolution (CDR) provides a vast network of informants across Cuba who spy on their neighbors for any signs of criticism or disloyalty to Castro or the revolution. This passage from *Waiting for Fidel*, by American journalist Christopher Hunt, describes the time he met the neighbor who spied on him during his residency in Cuba.

"There was no sneaking in or out of my building. A committee of no less than four noted my every move.

The pack's leader was a pudgy granny stationed opposite my front door. Up close, her face was a road map of tender lines. The crinkles multiplied when she smiled, which was often. But softness would be a perfect disguise, wouldn't it? So would the goodies she sold to neighbors beginning at seven A.M. every morning. Fruit puffs, sandwiches, coffee. . . . Who would suspect that the vendor was a spy?

Not I. Thus my surprise at Mrs. Guerra's first words to me: 'You're the American living in apartment 401.' Impressed, and intimidated, I asked for a coffee, which came in a plastic demitasse dented by tooth marks.

The old lady volunteered that she had lived on the block for decades. She pointed to a third-floor window behind the umbrella-covered table that served as her shop. Painted large on the wall to the left of the ground-floor entrance was a crest shaped like a shield. Thick vertical stripes of blue and white formed the bottom section. The top half was a man raising a sword above his head. Fat red letters said CDR. Smaller print spelled out Comite por la Defensa e la Revolucion.

The Committee for the Defense of the Revolution was a big reason for a foreigner to be edgy in Cuba. Every block, factory, and farm had a council to which Cubans reported anything out of the ordinary. Signs of excessive wealth rate a black mark. So did a neighbor caught bad-mouthing the government. Failing to inform was also a no-no. Irregularities were logged by the CDR. Serious infractions and strange people were reported to the security forces, who could turn a morning sighting into a midday arrest.

The CDR log labeled Mrs. Guerra's building the nerve center of the block's intelligence operations. The buck stopped here for the collective vigilance that Fidel Castro said was necessary."

The Dangers of Speaking Out

In this atmosphere of oppression, few people or groups openly oppose Castro. Cubans know that such opposition can result in reprisals in the form of imprisonment, fines, exile, loss of employment—or worse. Even those who are willing to risk reprisal have difficulty working together for reform. A culture of mistrust, bred by decades of spying and informing on one another, has resulted in people keeping to themselves rather than sharing their true opinions with other Cubans. As Carlos Alberto Montaner explains:

> Mutual distrust is one of the consistent elements of totalitarian societies, and the first thing families teach the children is to distrust and to pretend, for the child's chances of not running afoul of the repressive machinery [the abusive powers of government] will depend on his skills in those two behaviors. At the same time, that family training, the development of cynicism and lying as a means of protection, helps convince the child that the system is invincible and that it would be futile to try to oppose it. There is no sense in fighting. Survival is achieved by faking it. There is no point in running risks by defending dangerous principles. Sacrificing oneself for others—in a community of informers—would be idiocy.[85]

Even without the real threat of imprisonment or other reprisals, dissidents have limited means of protest at their disposal. They cannot run for office as members of opposition political parties, because there are no political parties besides the Communist Party. Nor can they openly and freely publish books, newspapers, or articles critical of the government, because such actions could be deemed illegal and punishable by government officials. For the most part, all they can do is circulate petitions, write articles that they distribute secretly, and grant interviews to foreign journalists.

Dissidents also find it hard to communicate with others. Paper and ink shortages, combined with old Soviet-era printing presses that tend to break down and for which spare parts are hard to find, make it difficult to publish their ideas. Making matters worse, the Cuban police usually confiscate fax machines and computers to prevent dissidents from sharing their ideas with one another and with the outside world.

For all these reasons, Castro's opponents tend to be isolated from one another and unable to coordinate their efforts. At most, some dissenters manage to form small independent groups that the state decisively dismisses as *grupos cculos* (little groups). The government claims that these groups are funded by criminal organizations in Miami that it calls the Cuban Mafia and uses this claim as another excuse to crack down on dissenters.

Cuba's Undaunted Dissenters

Many Cubans, however, refuse to be cowed by Castro. Over and over since Castro's takeover of Cuba, human rights advocates, reform-minded individuals, and opposition groups have arisen to demand political, economic, and social changes. Invariably, Castro has crushed them all. Castro's supporters approve of these crackdowns and say that Cuba's laws against illicit association give the regime the legitimacy the government needs to persecute dissidents.

In recent years the number of dissidents has been rising. Many of these protesters were involved with the Varela Project, a peti-

These supporters of the Varela Project, a project calling for sweeping political and civil reform, are some of Cuba's most prominent dissidents.

tion drive that called for political and civil reform. On May 10, 2002, leaders of the movement presented the petition, bearing eleven thousand signatures, to the National Assembly for consideration. The petition called for a national referendum that would let Cubans vote on political rights, free and open elections, freedom of the press, and other issues.

Since the Varela Project operated under petition guidelines guaranteed by the Cuban constitution, Castro could not charge the protesters with acting illegally. Instead the government struck back with its own petition. In a report on Cuba in 2003, the international watchdog organization Human Rights Watch observes:

In June, in what seemed like a distorted caricature of the earlier campaign, the authorities organized a mass signature collection effort in support of Cuba's socialist system. Holding marches all across the country, and employing many thousands of signature collectors, the government claimed to have gathered more than eight million signatures in two days. With this purported mandate, the National Assembly then proceeded to approve an official

Dissidence and Departure

proposal enshrining the socialist system in Cuba's constitution as "irrevocable."[86]

These actions made it all but impossible for the dissidents to seek change, even when they followed the rules imposed by Castro.

Several months later, Castro took harsher action against his newest critics. Police arrested several dissidents, including members of a group calling itself the Fraternal Brothers for Dignity Movement, human rights advocates, and independent journalists. Then in March 2003, Castro launched his biggest crackdown in years. Castro's men rounded up seventy-five dissenters, including leaders of the Varela Project, along with independent journalists, librarians, labor organizers, human rights activists, and others.

Ignoring protests and condemnations from human rights organizations and the governments of the United States and other countries, the Cuban government put the detainees on trial and sentenced many of them to anywhere from six to twenty-eight years in prison. Among other charges leveled at them, they were accused of accepting money from the United States—something the U.S. government denies. Cuban authorities claimed

Hector Palacios (seated), a leader of the Varela Project, was betrayed by fellow dissident Odilia Collazo (standing, center), who was actually a government agent.

the dissidents had violated a 1999 law forbidding nearly all forms of dissent.

Among those who testified during the court proceedings were people the dissidents knew well and had trusted. Hector Palacios, a leader of the Varela Project, was shocked when Odilia Collazo testified against him. Palacios had always thought of Collazo as the founder and president of the illegal Human Rights Party; but Collazo, it turned out, was also a government agent who had infiltrated the ranks of the dissident movement. Another infiltrator was a thirty-nine-year-old internist, Dr. Pedro Luis Veliz Martinez, who had spied on one of his neighbors involved with the outlawed opposition Liberal Party.

In yet another case, Marta Beatriz Roque, a respected economist and veteran opponent of Castro, was dismayed when the woman she thought was her close friend testified against her. The informer was Aleida Godinez, another Castro spy who had posed as both an independent journalist and a leader of the Assembly for the Promotion of Civil Society—a group of reformers. After the trial, Godinez gloated to the Associated Press, "The opposition is finished, it has ended, it will never lift its head again."[87]

Destroying dissent, however, may in the long run work against both the Cuban people and their oppressive government. As Barbara Robson notes, during Cuba's extraordinarily hard economic times

> the right to dissent, to have one's voice at least heard in complaint, if not in working towards solutions to social and economic problems becomes crucial. The government's suppression of dissent and emphasis on control, conformity and centralization is blocking initiative and innovation which could help address the country's problems. Many Cubans feel

that the only solution to their distress is to leave.[88]

When they do leave, they join a tragic outflow of humanity from the island that has been under way for decades.

Willing Exiles

Since Castro's takeover of the island, as many as 1 million Cubans have expressed their opposition to his dictatorial rule by leaving the country by almost any means possible. Today almost one out of every ten Cubans lives abroad; most of the exiles live in the United States. Dispirited and depressed by conditions in their own country, many Cubans feel enticed to leave their country by the lure of a better life in the United States. Their desire to flee is also fueled by conservative exile groups in Miami that encourage the departure of Cubans by funding organizations such as Brothers to the Rescue. In the mid-1990s, this Miami-based volunteer group sponsored flights by paramilitary pilots to rescue Cuban refugees who were escaping Cuba on the open sea. Over the years many Cubans have also received encouragement from the U.S. government. Cubans know that the United States has long opposed Castro and desires his removal from power. Every day, offshore broadcasts from U.S.-sponsored Radio Marti penetrates Cuban homes with news and anti-Castro propaganda that add to the discontent of many people. The United States also maintains a policy that welcomes as a refugee almost any Cuban who is literally able to touch soil in the United States. These refugees are eligible for refugee benefits, services, and other special privileges denied to immigrants from other countries. Such benefits serve as a powerful magnet to the poverty-stricken in Cuba.

Castro's brutal, repressive regime and his disregard for human rights, coupled with Cuba's ongoing economic hard times and widespread scarcity of food, medicine, and other necessities, work together to shove many Cubans from their native shores. Some Cuban analysts believe that Castro actually hopes to push dissidents away from Cuba's shores to permanently remove leaders of antigovernment movements.

Escaping in Waves

Although it is illegal to exit Cuba without permission, Cubans do so anyway, just as they have done in the past. Most exiles departed Cuba in three big waves. The first wave occurred in 1959 and the early 1960s. Many of these exiles were educated, skilled middle-class professional people and their families who understood what a Communist regime would mean to their well-being. The next wave took place between the mid-1960s and mid-1980s. Cubans who left during this time were generally working-class individuals. Unlike the first wave of refugees, many of these escapees were not particularly opposed to the revolution; instead they were dissatisfied that it had not lived up to their expectations. The hemorrhaging of human beings out of Cuba during this second wave became acute in 1979, when 120,000 people tried to leave. This time, Castro, as if to show his contempt, allowed most of them to leave. He even gave orders to open Cuban prisons and allow "antisocial elements"—dissidents, criminals, homosexuals, and others—to board boats headed for Florida.

Finally, as many as thirty-three thousand more Cubans left in the 1990s, after the Soviet Union collapsed and Cuba entered its Special Time of economic depression. Many of these escapees were *boleros* (raft people); who sneaked away from their country in crop dusters and on homemade boats, inner tubes, rafts, Styrofoam floats, and almost anything else that floated. Some even windsurfed their way to freedom.

That ingenuity has not ceased. In July 2003 twelve Cubans, in a classic use of *inventar y escapar*, made the ninety-mile trip across the Straits of Florida in a bright green 1951 flatbed Chevrolet truck attached to a pontoon made of fifty-five-gallon drums. The escapees attached a propeller to the driveshaft of the truck to propel the craft through the water.

All too often, Cubans lack proper supplies and equipment to build safe, navigable, well-stocked craft to make the journey to Florida or a Caribbean island safely. Many leave Cuba on impulse or hurry to escape before informers turn them in to authorities. Sadly, through the years, thousands have perished trying to flee Cuba, either dying from dehydration and hunger or drowning when their homemade raft falls apart. Sharks have devoured countless others. Their deaths continue to haunt their loved ones in Cuba. "Every Cuban also had a friend, or a friend of a neighbor who disappeared at sea,"[89] writes Christopher Hunt.

Cuban authorities try to capture those who flee and often punish the captives with fines and prison sentences. This use of force, combined with the hazards of thousands of unskilled people crossing the Straits of Florida in unsafe boats and rafts, has meant that only an estimated 25 to 33 percent of those who flee Cuba illegally actually make it safely to the United States.

The governments of both Cuba and the United States recognize the dangers of these desperate attempts and have taken steps to curb them. As a result of recent negotiations between the United States and Cuba, the days of unregulated, mass migrations to Florida on dangerous boats have come to an end, at least for a while. As part of the new agreements, the United States has promised to allow at least twenty thousand Cubans to immigrate legally every year. Meanwhile, in Cuba, a government-controlled lottery determines who those twenty thousand individuals will be. However, according to American conservative commentator Ivan G. Osorio, this step is "a move that puts potential emigrants at the mercy of the Castro government, which can issue or deny exit permits for any reason Castro's henchmen see fit. Even worse, those asking permission to leave are often branded as counterrevolutionaries and subjected to a variety of reprisals."[90]

Another problem is that the United States does not always accept twenty thousand Cubans every year. In 2002, for example, only eighteen thousand Cubans were allowed into the country.

Most likely, the twenty thousand figure vastly underrepresents the number of Cubans wishing to flee. According to unofficial estimates made by foreign diplomats working in Cuba, at least half of Cuba's population would leave Cuba if they had the chance. In fact, in spite of the new arrangement, many Cubans still try to enter the United States illegally. Those who are caught at sea are generally returned to Cuba. Some Cubans are so desperate to leave that they resort to illegal, if not criminal, measures to escape. They have stolen boats or hijacked planes to make the

Twelve Cubans tried to escape Cuba in July 2003 in a raft made from an old truck. Since 1959 thousands of Cubans have made desperate attempts to reach the United States.

Eyewitness to the Sinking of the *13th of March* Tugboat

This extract from the testimony of Janette Hernandez Gutierrez, a passenger on the *13th of March* tugboat, given to an unofficial human rights group in Cuba shortly after the attack, appears in a special report on the incident prepared by Amnesty International, the well-known human rights organization.

"As we were leaving the bay, we saw two tugboats at the mouth of the bay. As we left, they also left and started directing jets of water at us. Constantly. They would not stop, even though they knew there were children on board. . . . The pressurized water jets were really powerful. We were holding the children, afraid that they would fall. The men were standing behind us, afraid that we would fall. But so that they would see that there were women and children on board, we had to go out on deck, so that they would be certain of that and would not commit murder. . . . At no time did they shoot at us neither did they at any time order us to halt with the loudspeaker. They simply let us leave the bay and attacked us seven miles out where there are no witnesses. . . . They sent one of the tugboats, the biggest one, which was green with a red line along it, behind us and it hit us from the stern and broke our boat in half. . . . When that happened the boat started to drift because the captain . . . was forced into the sea from the pressure of the water jets. . . . He disappeared just like that and when Raúl saw that we were drifting, he assumed responsibility and ran upstairs. . . . By then we knew we were going to sink, it was something I just knew, I had a feeling they were going to kill us because otherwise they would have stopped. Raúl stopped the engine . . . and when they saw that Raúl had stopped it, they did not forgive that or respect what Raúl did. They sank us in the following way: the tugboat which had split our stern went ahead and split us from the prow. That meant there was no way to keep the tugboat afloat, it was sinking, because the weight was all in the middle. . . . But they did not throw us lifebelts or try to help us in any way. . . . Then a "griffin" [coast guard vessel] arrived, it was the only one which helped us by throwing us lifebelts but the tugboats stood by doing nothing, they did not help at all. Later a small speedboat arrived and picked up about seven people."

trip to freedom. The U.S. government, though reluctant to return anyone to a totalitarian dictatorship, generally has little sympathy for those who commit piracy and sends accused hijackers back to Cuba. Once back in Cuba, they often face severe reprisals. In April 2003, for example, a government firing squad executed three men convicted of hijacking a boat with the purpose of fleeing Cuba.

Critics of the immigration agreement say that it will do little to curb dangerous attempts at freedom as long as American policy makers continue to grant haven to any Cuban who is literally able to set foot on American soil. Writes Ivan G. Osorio, "The change in the law stemmed the flow of rafters temporarily, but it did not stop Cubans from trying to cross the Florida Straits. Rather, it created a thriving new black market: human smuggling. Smugglers charge as much as $10,000 a person for the crossing, a prohibitive sum for most Cubans."[91] Cuban authorities impose stiff penalties on those caught in attempts to smuggle human beings out of Cuba. When Castro's police apprehended one family negotiating with smugglers to help them escape Cuba in 2001, they jailed the father and seized the entire family's life savings.

A Nation with a Broken Heart

No matter what their views on Castro, most Cubans are saddened when their friends and relatives depart the land of their birth, sometimes without ever saying good-bye. Both those who leave and those who are left behind realize all too well that they may never see one another again. Though many Cuban exiles love being in the United States and wish never to return to Cuba, others miss their native land and Cuban culture. Meanwhile, in Cuba, many of those left behind become frustrated and angry that they cannot leave too. Believing that the future of Cuba under Castro is bleak and without hope, many Cuban parents hope their daughters marry foreigners and move abroad or encourage their children to immigrate to the United States for a better future, even if that means never seeing them again.

When Fidel Is Gone

For years, exiled Cubans in the United States have been planning on returning to Cuba and launching a new revolution when Castro dies. Although he is now seventy-three and in apparent good health, Castro cannot last too many more years as an effective leader. Many Cubans think that when death or poor health conquers him, his Socialist rule will collapse. Then and only then will Cuba be free to redefine itself and try again to create a new paradise in the Caribbean.

Notes

Introduction: Cuba: A Troubled Paradise

1. Christopher Hunt, *Waiting for Fidel.* Boston: Houghton Mifflin, 1998, p. 253.

Chapter 1: Living Under the Heel of Fidel Castro

2. The Cuban constitution, Article 33, http://members.fortunecity.com/stalin mao/cuba/documents/constitution.html #TitleIV.
3. The Cuban constitution, Article 102.
4. Isadora Tattlin, *Cuba Diaries: An American Housewife in Havana.* Chapel Hill, NC: Algonquin Books, 2002, p. 131.
5. Interview with Manuel Caberio, August 30, 2003.
6. Quoted in Christopher P. Baker, *Mi Moto Fidel.* Washington, DC: National Geographic, 2001, p. 178.
7. Tony Mendoza, *Cuba—Going Back.* Austin: University of Texas Press, 1999 p. 75.
8. Interview with Omar, August 29, 2003.
9. Tattlin, *Cuba Diaries*, p. 104.
10. Hunt, *Waiting for Fidel*, p. 186.
11. Catherine Moses, *Real Life in Castro's Cuba.* Wilmington, DE: SR Books, 2000, p. 23.

Chapter 2: Getting By in Castro's Cuba: *No Es Fácil* (It Is Not Easy)

12. Interview with Angelica, September 19, 2003.
13. Interview with Flora, August 25, 2003.
14. Interview with Omar, August 25, 2003.
15. Hunt, *Waiting for Fidel*, p. 73.
16. Tanja Sturm, "Cuban Healthcare in the Twenty-First Century. Does It Work?" *Focus 2000*, World Market Research Centre, www.worldmarketsanalysis.com/ InFocus2002/articles/americas_Cuba_ health.html.
17. Eugen Linden, "The Nature of Cuba," *Smithsonian*, May 2003, p. 98.
18. Quoted in Henry Shukman, "Making Music," in *Cuba: True Stories*, ed. Tom Miller, San Francisco: Travelers' Tales, 2001, p. 58.
19. Quoted in Mark Cramer, *Culture Shock, Cuba.* Portland, OR: Graphic Arts Center, 2000, p. 122.
20. Interview with Manuel Caberio, August 30, 2003.
21. Interview with a former resident of Cuba, August 17, 2001.

Chapter 3: Getting Along in Cuba: Social Structure and Human Relationships

22. Mona Rosendahl, *Inside the Revolution: Everyday Life in Socialist Cuba.* Ithaca, NY: Cornell University Press, 1997, p. 111.
23. Linden, "The Nature of Cuba," pp. 97–98.
24. Quoted in Cramer, *Culture Shock, Cuba*, p. 146.
25. Quoted in Hunt, *Waiting for Fidel*, p. 87.
26. Lynn Darling, "Havana at Midnight," in *Cuba: True Stories*, ed. Tom Miller, p. 261.
27. Rosendahl, *Inside the Revolution*, p. 160.
28. Cramer, *Culture Shock, Cuba*, p. 69.
29. Cramer, *Culture Shock, Cuba*, p. 78.
30. Moses, *Real Life in Castro's Cuba*, p. 147.

31. Barbara Robson, "The Cubans Their History and Culture: Refugee Fact Sheet Series No. 12," U.S. Refugee Program, April 25, 2000. http://culturalorientation.net/Cubans/CUBANS.HTM.
32. Rosendahl, *Inside the Revolution*, p. 71.
33. Cramer, *Culture Shock, Cuba*, p. 133.
34. The Cuban constitution, Article 20.
35. Robson, "The Cubans Their History and Culture."
36. Interview with Marti Walstad, September 2, 2003.
37. Rosendahl, *Inside the Revolution*, p. 178.

Chapter 4: Literacy for All, Castro Style

38. Christopher P. Baker, *Cuba Handbook*. Chico, CA: Moon, 1997, p. 106.
39. Quoted in Damarys Ocaña, "Study, Work, Rifle," *Miami Herald*, August 6, 2000. www.geocities.com/sccgsnow/articles/school.htm.
40. Robson, "The Cubans Their History and Culture."
41. Net for Cuba, "Study, Work, Rifle: Cuba's Educational System Presses Revolutionary Message Along with ABC's," Documents and Letters, www.netforcuba.org/documentsandletters06.htm.
42. Agustín Blázquez and Jaums Sutton, "Education in Elian's Cuba: What Americans Don't Know," No Castro Nor His Regime, March 19, 2000. www.nocastro.com/archives/elian52.htm.
43. Interview with Julie, August 25, 2003.
44. Bureau of Western Hemisphere Affairs, "Intellectual and Academic Freedom in Cuba," U.S. Department of State Fact Sheet, Washington, DC, September 13, 2001. www.state.gov/p/wha/rls/fs/2001/fsjulydec/4890.htm.
45. Tattlin, *Cuban Diaries*, p. 80.
46. Interview with Julie, August 25, 2003.
47. Moses, *Real Life in Castro's Cuba*, p. 71.

Chapter 5: Trying to Stay Healthy

48. Robson, "The Cubans Their History and Culture."
49. Interview with an American traveler to Cuba who wishes to conceal her identity, September 2001.
50. Sturm, "Cuban Healthcare in the Twenty-First Century."
51. Quoted in Barbara Jamison, "Alternative Health Care Flourishes in the Caribbean," Alternative Health Care, September 30, 2002. http://blueprint.bluecrossmn.com/topic/cuba.
52. Quoted in Carol Canter, "Commitment to Care: Nurses in Cuba Offer a Glimpse into the Island Republic's Health System," Nurseweek.com, Global Exchange, June 11, 2001. www.globalexchange.org/countries/cuba/sustainable/nursecare061101.html.
53. Jamison, "Alternative Health Care Flourishes in the Caribbean."
54. Jamison, "Alternative Health Care Flourishes in the Caribbean."
55. Moses, *Real Life in Castro's Cuba*, pp. 67–68.
56. Interview with Flora, August 25, 2003.
57. Miquel A. Faria Jr., "Socialized Medicine in Cuba (2002)—Part II: Other Hidden Faces of Cuban Medicine," Newsmax.com, August 20, 2002. www.newsmax.com/archives/articles/2002/8/25/ 220915.shtml.
58. Hilda Molina, "Cuban Medicine Today," April 17, 2003. www.cubacenter.org/media/archives/1998/summer/medicine_today.php3
59. Tattlin, *Cuba Diaries*, p. 42.

Chapter 6: Seeking an Escape in Leisure Time

60. Rosendahl, *Inside the Revolution*, p. 47.
61. Mendoza, *Cuba—Going Back*, p. 111.
62. Kirsten Ellis, *Traveler's Cuba Companion.* Old Saybrook, CT: Globe Pequot Press, 1999, p. 65.
63. Interview with Julie, August 25, 2003.
64. Mendoza, *Cuba—Going Back*, p. 130.
65. Quoted in Ken Schulman "Sports in Cuba: The System," Trustees of Boston University, 2002. http://archives.onlya game.org/onlinefeatures/cuba1.shtml.
66. Quoted in Mike Sandrock, "Big Hearts in Havana," *Footnotes,* Road Runners Club of America, www.rrca.org/publicat/ havana.html.
67. Andrew Cawthorne, "Vibrant Cuban Drama Dares to Question," Reuters, October 21, 1998. http://64.21.33.164/ CNews/y98/Oct98/21e8.htm.
68. Cawthorne, "Vibrant Cuban Drama Dares to Question."
69. Cawthorne, "Vibrant Cuban Drama Dares to Question."
70. Quoted in Cuba.ru.www.cuba.ru/index. php3?id_ rubr=1217.
71. Ellis, *Traveler's Cuba Companion*, p. 84.
72. Quoted in Stephen Smith, "The House of Tango," *Cuba: True Stories,* ed. Tom Miller, p. 102.
73. Quoted in Nick Caistor, "Heberto Padilla: Poetic Symbol of Intellectual Repression in Castro's Cuba," *Guardian Unlimited*, October 14, 2000. www. guardian.co.uk/cuba/story/0,11983,7127 16,00.html.

Chapter 7: Buoying the Cuban Spirit

74. John W. Kennedy, "Cuba's Next Revolution: How Christians Are Reshaping Castro's Communist Stronghold," *Chris-tianity Today*, January 12, 1998. www. christianitytoday.com/ct/8t1/8t1018.html.
75. Moses, *Real Life in Castro's Cuba,* p. 156.
76. Moses, *Real Life in Castro's Cuba,* p. 157.
77. Quoted in Dan Freedman, "Cuban Jews Survive Years in the Revolutionary Desert," Hearst Newspapers, 2000. http://jewishcuba.org/freedman.html.
78. Interview with Angelica, September 20, 2003.
79. Interview with Manuel Caberio, August 30, 2003.
80. U.S. Department of State, Bureau of Democracy, Human Rights, and Labor, Bureau of Public Affairs, "International Religious Freedom Report 2002," October 7, 2002. www.state.gov/g/drl/rls/irf/ 2002/14039.htm.
81. Quoted in Mark Albrecht, "Life in Cuba," World Evangelical Alliance, Religious Liberty E-Mail Conference, January 3, 2002. www.wordevangelical.org/ persec_cuba_03jan02.html.

Chapter 8: Dissidence and Departure

82. Carlos Alberto Montaner, *Journey to the Heart of Cuba: Life as Fidel Castro.* New York: Algora, 2001, p. 90.
83. U.S. Department of State, Bureau of Democracy, Human Rights, and Labor, "Country Reports on Human Rights Practices—2002: Cuba," March 31, 2003. http://64.21.33.164/ref/dis/040103 01.htm.
84. Amnesty International, "Cuba," in *Report 2003.* http://web.amnesty.org/report2003/ cub-summary.eng.
85. Montaner, *Journey to the Heart of Cuba*, p. 132.

86. Human Rights Watch, "Human Rights Watch Report 2003 on Cuba," www.hrw.org/wr2k3/america5.html.

87. Quoted in CBS News Online, "Cuban Spy Taunts Opposition," April 22, 2003. www.cbsnews.com/stories/2003/04/22/world/main550591.shtml.

88. Robson, "The Cubans Their History and Culture."

89. Hunt, *Waiting for Fidel*, p. 177.

90. Ivan G. Osorio, "Stop Sending Cubans Back to Castro's Gulag: Bush Should Repeal Clinton's 'Wet Feet–Dry Feet' Policy," *National Review Online*, April 2003. www.nationalreview.com/comment/comment-osorio041703.asp.

91. Osorio, "Stop Sending Cubans Back to Castro's Gulag."

For Further Reading

Lisa Ballinger, *The Importance of Fidel Castro.* San Diego: Lucent, 2003. Supported with numerous extended quotes, this biography traces the rise of Castro from revolutionary leader to committed Communist dictator.

Clifford W. Crouch, *Cuba.* Philadelphia: Chelsea House, 1999. Informative and readable, this book focuses on Cuban history and how Castro seized power.

Sean Sheehan, *Cuba.* New York: Marshall Cavendish, 1999. Richly illustrated with color photographs, this book provides up-to-date descriptions of various aspects of Cuban culture, though it minimizes the impact of Castro's dictatorial rule.

Works Consulted

Books

Christopher P. Baker, *Cuba Handbook.* Chico, CA: Moon, 1997. This hefty, readable travel book is packed with interesting facts about almost every aspect of Cuban life.

———, *Mi Moto Fidel.* Washington, DC: National Geographic, 2001. A lively travelogue of a British author's motorcycle trip through Cuba. Readable and informative, though some parts may not be suitable for young readers.

Giselle Balido, *Cubantime: A Celebration of Cuban Life in America.* New York: Silver Lining Books, 2001. Beautifully illustrated with vivid color photography, and text in both English and Spanish that explores the lives of Cuba's exiles in the United States.

Miquel Barnet, *Afro-Cuban Religions*, Trans. Christine Renata Ayorinde. Princeton, NJ: Markus Wiener, 2001. A scholarly guide to Afro-Cuban religions.

Mark Cramer, *Culture Shock, Cuba.* Portland, OR: Graphic Arts Center, 2000. A concise and interesting travelogue about Cuba by an experienced American traveler. Beautifully illustrated and readable, this book offers useful insights into aspects of life in contemporary Cuba.

Andrei Codrescu, *Ay Cuba!* New York: St. Martin's Press, 1999. Poet Codrescu provides a colorful account of street life in modern Cuba, some of which may not be appropriate for all young adults.

Kirsten Ellis, *Traveler's Cuba Companion.* Old Saybrook, CT: Globe Pequot Press, 1999.

Maurice Halperin, *Return to Havana: The Decline of Cuban Society Under Castro.* Nashville, TN: Vanderbilt University Press, 1994. A scholarly appraisal of Castro's impact on Cuban society written by an American scholar who has taught and lived in Cuba.

Christopher Hunt, *Waiting for Fidel:* Boston: Houghton Mifflin, 1998. This book, by an American traveler to Cuba, offers interesting and poignant glimpses into the lives of hundreds of Cubans.

Llilian Llanes, *The Houses of Old Cuba.* New York: Thames & Hudson, 1999. An interesting book with vivid photographs that explores the history and architecture of Cuban homes and how they affect the lives of Cubans.

Tony Mendoza, *Cuba—Going Back.* Austin: University of Texas Press, 1999. A personal account by a Cuban American who returned to the land of his birth.

Tom Miller, ed., *Cuba: True Stories.* San Francisco: Travelers' Tales, 2001. A collection of essays and travel stories about Cuba.

Carlos Alberto Montaner, *Journey to the Heart of Cuba: Life as Fidel Castro.* New York: Algora, 2001. A well-written history and critical analysis of Castro's Cuba.

Catherine Moses, *Real Life in Castro's Cuba.* Wilmington, DE: SR Books, 2000. A readable and informative book by a U.S. press secretary and spokesperson who worked in Cuba for two years. Provides a frank and disturbing picture of life in Cuba.

Mona Rosendahl, *Inside the Revolution: Everyday Life in Socialist Cuba.* Ithaca, NY: Cornell University Press, 1997. A fascinating and very readable work by a

Swedish social anthropologist who lived in Cuba, where she researched aspects of Cuban society.

Pedro Pérez Sarduy and Jean Stubbs, eds., *Afro-Cuban Voices: On Race and Identity in Contemporary Cuba.* Gainesville: University Press of Florida, 2000.

Isadora Tattlin, *Cuba Diaries: An American Housewife in Havana.* Chapel Hill, NC: Algonquin Books, 2002. Tattlin's diaries of her years in Cuba provide colorful and anecdotal glimpses into everyday life in Cuba.

Jacobo Timmerman, *Cuba: A Journey.* Trans. Toby Talbot. New York: Alfred A. Knopf, 1990. A compilation of encounters with various Cubans by a renowned Argentine journalist.

Armando Valladares, *Against All Hope: The Prison Memoirs of Armando Valladares.* Trans. Andrew Hurley. New York: Alfred A. Knopf, 1986. Valladares gives a powerful and horrifying account of his twenty-two years as a political prisoner in a Cuban prison.

Periodical

Eugen Linden, "The Nature of Cuba," *Smithsonian*, May 2003.

Internet Sources

"ABCs of Cuban Music," www.azureva.com/gb/cuba/magazine/musique.php3.

Mark Albrecht, "Life in Cuba," World Evangelical Alliance, Religious Liberty E-Mail Conference, January 3, 2002. www.worldevangelical.org/persec_cuba_03jan02.html.

Amnesty International, "Report 2003 Cuba," http://web.amnesty.org/report2003/cub-summary-eng.

———, "The Sinking of the '13 de Marzo' Tugboat on 13 July 1994," http://web.amnesty.org/library/index/ENGAMR250131997.

Agustín Blázquez and Jaums Sutton, "Education in Elian's Cuba: What Americans Don't Know," No Castro Nor His Regime, March 19, 2000. www.nocastro.com/archives/elian52.htm.

Bureau of Western Hemisphere Affairs, "Intellectual and Academic Freedom in Cuba," U.S. Department of State Fact Sheet, Washington, DC, September 13, 2001. www.state.gov/p/wha/rls/fs/2001/fsjulydec/4890.html.

Nick Caistor, "Heberto Padilla: Poetic Symbol of Intellectual Repression in Castro's Cuba." *Guardian,* October 14, 2000. www.guardian.co.uk/cuba/story/0,11983,712716,00.html.

Carol Canter, "Commitment to Care: Nurses in Cuba Offer a Glimpse into the Island Republic's Health System," Nurseweek.com, Global Exchange, June 11, 2001. www.globalexchange.org/countries/cuba/sustainable/nursecare061101.html.

Fidel Castro, "May Day 2003," Canadian Network on Cuba, May 1, 2003. www.canadiannetworkoncuba.ca/Documents/Fidel-MD2003.shtml.

Andrew Cawthorne, "Vibrant Cuban Drama Dares to Question," Reuters, October 21, 1998. http://64.21.33.164/CNews/y98/Oct98/21e8.htm.

CBS News Online, "Cuban Spy Taunts Opposition," April 22, 2003. www.cbsnews.com/stories/2003/04/22/world/main550591.shtml.

Oswaldo de Cespedes, "Public Healthcare in Cuba: A Challenge for the Future," Cubanet, November 19, 1998. http://64.21.33.164/CNews/y98/nov98/19e1.htm.

The Cuban constitution. http://members.

fortunecity.com/stalinmao/cuba/documents/constitution.html#TitleIV.

Tracey Easton, "In Cuba Soap Operas Can Be a Soapbox," *Dallas Morning News,* http://havanajournal.com/culture-comments/p608-0-3-0-1.

Miquel A. Faria Jr., "Socialized Medicine in Cuba (2002)—Part II: Other Hidden Faces of Cuban Medicine," Newsmax.com, August 20, 2002. www.newsmax.com/archives/articles/2002/8/25/220915.shtml.

Dan Freedman, "Cuban Jews Survive Years in the Revolutionary Desert," Hearst Newspapers, 2000. http://jewishcuba.org/freedman.html.

Human Rights Watch, "Human Rights Watch Report 2003 on Cuba." www.hrw.org/wr2k3/america5.html.

International Christian Concern, "A Report on Religious Persecution in Cuba." www.persecution.org/Countries/cuba.html#Articles.

Barbara Jamison, "Alternative Health Care Flourishes in the Caribbean," Alternative Health Care, September 3, 2002. http://blueprint.bluecrossmn.com/topic/cuba.

John W. Kennedy, "Cuba's Next Revolution: How Christians Are Reshaping Castro's Communist Stronghold," *Christianity Today*, January 12, 1998. www.christianitytoday.com/ct/8t1/8t1018.html.

Patricia Linderman, "Doctors for Dollars," *American Diplomacy*, Autumn 1999. www.unc.edu/depts/diplomat/AD_Issues-Andapl_13/linderman_cuba.html.

Hilda Molina, "Cuban Medicine Today," April 17, 2003. www.cubacenter.org/media/archives/1998/summer/medicine_today.

Sayli Navarro, "CUBA: Letter from a Dissident's Daughter Perico, Matanzas," Cuba Infolinks News and Information Services, March 28, 2003. www.cubainfolinks.net/Articles-2/letter_perico.htm.

"Study, Work, Rifle: Cuba's Educational System Presses Revolutionary Message Along with ABC's," Documents and Letters, Net for Cuba. www.netforcuba.org/documentsandletters06.htm.

Damarys Ocaña, "Study, Work, Rifle," *Miami Herald*, August 6, 2000. www.geocities.com/sccgsnow/articles/school.htm.

Ivan G. Osorio, "Stop Sending Cubans Back to Castro's Gulag: Bush Should Repeal Clinton's 'Wet Feet–Dry Feet' Policy," *National Review Online*, April 2003. www.nationalreview.com/comment/comment-osorio041703.asp.

Barbara Robson, "The Cubans Their History and Culture: Refugee Fact Sheet Series No 12," U.S. Refugee Program, April 25, 2000. http://culturalorientation.net/Cubans/CUBANS. HTM.

Mike Sandrock, "Big Hearts in Havana," *Footnotes*, Road Runners Club of America, www.rrca.org/publicat/havana.html.

Ken Schulman, "Sports in Cuba: The System," Trustees of Boston University, 2002. http://archives.onlyagame.org/onlinefeatures/cuba1.shtml.

Tanja Sturm, "Cuban Healthcare in the Twenty-First Century. Does It Work?" *Focus 2000*, World Market Research Centre, www.worldmarketsanalysis.com/InFocus2002/articles/americas_Cuba_health.html.

Giles Tremlett, "Dollar Gnaws at Cuba's Marvelous Revolution," *Guardian,* July 22, 2003. www.guardian.co.uk/print/0,3858,4717231-103681,00.html.

United Press International, "Cuba's AIDS Policy Offers Lessons," 2003. www.applesforhealth.com/GlobalHealth/cubaidpolo4.html.

U.S. Department of State, Bureau of Democracy, Human Rights, and Labor, Bureau of Public Affairs, "International Religious Freedom Report 2002," October 7, 2002.

www.state.gov/g/drl/rls/irf/2002/14039.htm.

U.S. Department of State, Bureau of Democracy, Human Rights, and Labor, "Country Reports on Human Rights Practices—2002: Cuba," March 31, 2003. http://64.21.33.164/ref/dis/04010301.htm.

Web Site

Cuba.ru (www.cuba.ru). This Web site is a rich source of information on Cuban culture, history, and geography. Articles are available in English, Spanish, and Russian.

Index

abortions, 37
acupuncture, 60
Africa, 10
Afro-Cuban religions, 74
AIDS, 56–57, 59
alternative medicine, 60
   see also health-care system;
    medicine, shortage of
Ana Betancourt School, 47
anesthetics, 60
Angola, 10
antibiotics, 59
anti-Fidelistos, 38
   see also opposition
antirevolutionary activity, 13,
   15–18, 41, 50, 86–92
anti-Semitism, 79–80
antisocial elements. *See*
   dissidents
army, 8–9, 34, 39
   see also military training;
    police
art, 73–74
Article 33 (constitution), 12
Assembly for the Promotion of
   Civil Society, 91
atheism, 76
   see also religion
athletic training, 68
automobiles, 24, 28, 58, 85

bandages, shortage of, 59
Baptist churches, 79
barter, 24–25, 32
baseball, 64, 66–67
Batista, Fulgencio, 8, 32
Bay of Pigs invasion, 8
beriberi (disease), 57
bicycles, 24, 34, 58
birth control, 37
blackmail, 16

black market, 25–26, 43, 53,
   60, 94–95
black people, 33, 39–40
Bolivia, 10, 46
boxing, 66
Brothers to the Rescue, 91
buddy system, 36
buses, 25, 85
businesses, 8, 26–27

capitalism, 9–10, 27, 46
Caribbean region, 10
Carnival, 69
carriages, horse-drawn, 24
cars. *See* automobiles
casa de la cultura, 71
casa de la trova, 71
Castro, Fidel
   dictatorship of, 8–21, 32
   opinions about, 38, 41, 44,
    95
   personality cult of, 46, 77
   revolution led by, 8–11
Catholic Church, 70, 76,
   78–79, 81–82
censorship, 12, 52, 70, 73–75,
   87–88
   see also media, government
    control of
change, fear of, 19, 21
children, 15–16, 36, 45–47
China, 58
Christianity, revival of, 77–79,
   81
Christmas, 70
churches. *See* religion
clothing, shortage of, 11, 22
Cobre, El, 82–83
Collazo, Odilia, 91
Columbia (dance), 73

Committee for the Defense of
   the Revolution (CDR),
   15–16, 36, 87
Communist Party, 9–10, 12–15,
   19–20, 32, 73
   loyalty to, 45, 49–50
   membership in, 18, 36,
    40–42, 47, 60, 62, 76
   see also Socialist state
Communist state, Cuba as,
   8–9, 85–86
community, sense of, 34–37
community-based clinics, 56,
   59
community leaders, spying on,
   15
community service, 36, 45, 49
Conference of Catholic
   Bishops, 79
Congo, 10
Congolese music, 73
constitution, 12–13, 34, 39, 76,
   89–90
consultario. See community-
   based clinics
conversation, love of, 34–36,
   44, 64–65, 71–72
Cooder, Ry, 73
Council of State, 12
counterrevolutionaries. *See*
   antirevolutionary activity;
   dissidents
country schools, 48
crime, 25–26, 86
criticism, constructive
   need for, 52–53, 75, 91
   not permitted, 13, 15
Cuba AIDS Project, 57
Cubanacan Tourism and
   Health, 61

Cuban Council of Churches, 77–78
Cuban Mafia, 88
Cuban-ness, 23–26, 33–36, 40–41, 64
cultural identity, 40–41
Cumulative Academic Record, 45–46
currency, foreign, 27, 31

dance, 65, 69–71, 73
day-care centers, 37, 39
defectors, 67, 75
    see also exiles
dentists, wages of, 53
depression, economic. See Special Time
dictatorship, 8–21, 32
diphtheria, elimination of, 54
discrimination, sexual. See gender equality
dissidents, 8, 13–14, 16, 73, 85–92
distrust, atmosphere of, 88
divorce, 38–39
doctors, 34, 36, 55–56, 59
    exile of, 8, 54, 61, 87
    surplus of, 50, 52
    wages of, 29, 32, 53, 63, 79
dollar economy, 26–29, 31, 40, 42–43, 52–53, 60, 68
    see also economy
dossiers, 16–17, 45–46
double-morals, 64–65
dual morality, 19
due process, denial of, 87
    see also judicial system

Easter, 70
economists, 55, 87, 91
economy, 12, 34
    problems with, 21–31, 44, 58–60, 77–78, 85, 91–92
    see also dollar economy
educational system, 10, 12, 16, 18–19, 34, 41, 44–54, 76

for health care, 56
    religious, 78–79
elections, 14
electricity, shortage of, 24
elementary schools, 46
embargo, by United States, 8, 10, 60, 68, 73
employment, 12, 18, 25, 31, 41
    loss of, 15–17, 87
engineers, 8, 50, 52–53
English language, 47
entrepreneurs. See self-employment
environmental problems, 58
equality, 32–34, 36, 41–43, 79
Ethiopia, 10
executions, 8, 14, 86, 94
exiles, 8, 19, 31, 38, 44, 86–95
    see also defectors
exports, 22
    see also sugar crop

Family Doctor Program, 56
family life, 36–39
farmers, 23, 26, 34
farms, 8
festivals, 34, 69–70, 80
Fiesta del Quince, La, 70
firing squads, 8, 94
folk art, 74
food, shortage of, 10–11, 22–23, 51–52, 57–60, 69, 79–80, 92
foreign aid, 27–28, 31, 76–77
foreigners
    contact with, suppressed, 12
    medical care for, 36, 54–55, 60–63
foreign policy, 13
Fraternal Brothers for Dignity Movement, 90
freedom, lack of, 41–43, 87
    see also repression
free enterprise, 27
    see also dollar economy; self-employment

fuel, shortage of, 10–11, 24, 28, 58
future, 11, 19–21, 34, 95

garbage pick-up, 57, 59
gasoline. See fuel, shortage of
gender equality, 33, 39, 79
gifts, 38, 42
God, belief in discouraged, 46
Godinez, Aleida, 91
government
    basic needs provided by, 15, 18–19, 22, 32–33, 40–42, 71
    local, 34
    reduction of services by, 22, 57–61
    total control by, 8–10, 12–21, 26–28, 36–38, 75, 86
    see also health-care system; media, government control of
Granma, El, (newspaper), 14
Great Britain, 54
Grenada, 10
Guatemala, 8
Guevara, Ernesto "Che," 46, 74
Guitar Festival, 71

Haiti, 81
Havana (Cuba)
    health care in, 60
    life in, 28, 34–36, 42, 59, 64, 71
Havana Jazz Festival, 71
Havana Varadero Beach, 29
health-care system, 9, 34, 41, 54–63, 70
hepatitis, 59
herbal remedies, 60
higher education, 49–50
    see also universities
high schools, 46–47
hijackers, 93–94
HIV, 56–57, 59

holidays, 69–70
hospitals, 56, 59–60
Hot Corner (Havana), 64
house churches, 85
housing, 41
    shortage of, 24, 37, 59
human relationships, 32–43
human rights, violations of, 57, 76, 86–88, 90, 92
Human Rights Party, 91
hunger, 58

Ideal Place, The (play), 70
immigration agreement, 92–94
immunizations, 54, 56
imperialism, 46
indoctrination, 41, 45–47, 50, 52–53
infant mortality rate, 54, 59
infiltration. *See* spy system
informants. *See* spy system
intellectuals, repression of, 16, 52–53
International Ballet Festival, 71
International Festival of New Latin-American Cinema, 71
International Lyric Festival, 71
Internet, 19
Italy, 52, 67

jai alai, 66
jam sessions, 73
jazz, 73
jobs. *See* employment
John Paul II (pope), visit by, 76, 78
joint business ventures, 27
    see also economy; foreign aid
jokes, 64–65
journalists, persecution of, 87, 90
    see also media, government control of
Judaism, 79–80
judicial system, 13–14, 86–87

labor organizers, persecution of, 90
Latin America, 32, 38–39, 50
    Communist insurgencies in, 8, 10
    infant mortality rate in, 54
    school systems in, 44, 52
lawyers, persecution of, 87
legislature, 13
leisure activities, 12, 64–75
Lenin, Vladimir, 8
    see also Marxist-Leninist theory
leptospirosis (disease), 57
Liberal Party, 91
librarians, persecution of, 90
life expectancy, 54, 59
lines, waiting in, 23–24
literacy, 10, 44–53
little groups, 88
loyalists, 13, 17–18, 38
    see also Communist Party, loyalty to; Revolution (1959), loyalty to
Lucumi religion, 80–81

machismo, 39
malaria, elimination of, 54
malnutrition, 57–59
marriage, 38–39
Marx, Karl, 8
Marxist-Leninist theory, 32, 77
May Day, 69
measles, 54
media, government control of, 9, 12–14, 19, 65–66, 87
    see also censorship
medical facilities. *See* community-based clinics; hospitals; polyclinics
medical schools, 54
medical tourism, 61–63
medicine, 19, 32
    shortage of, 11, 22, 54–55, 59–60, 92
    see also health-care system

men, status of, 39
    see also women, status of
Miami, Florida, 91
middle class, 33, 50
middle schools, 46–47
migrations, mass, 92–93
    see also exiles
military training, 36, 46, 49
Ministry of the Interior, 16, 85
money, shortage of, 22, 24
moonlighting, 25–26, 30, 33
music, 28, 65, 71–73
mysticism, 81–82

National Assembly of the People's Power, 12
National Ballet, 71
National Symphony Orchestra, 71
neighborhoods, 34–36
neuritis (disease), 57
nurses, 8, 54–55
nutrition, inadequate, 57–59

Old Havana, 28
    see also Havana
Olympic Games, 67–68
on-the-job training, 49
opposition, 13, 15–18, 41, 50, 86–92
Other Tempest, The (play), 70

Palacios, Hector, 91
Pentecostal churches, 79
performing arts, 70–72
persecution. *See* prisoners, political; punishment; repression
peso economy, 42–43
    see also dollar economy
petition drives, 88–91
pharmacies, 60
pharmacists, 55
physicians. *See* doctors
Pioneros (Pioneers), 46
Playa Girón (Cuba), 29

plays, 70
police, 9, 13, 15
   see also army
polio, 54
Politburo, 12
political parties, repression of, 9, 13–14, 88
pollution, 58
polyclinics, 56
poster art, 74
poverty, 11, 28, 34, 43–44, 50, 52, 91
power outages, 22, 24
preventive medicine, 56, 59
prisoners, political, 8, 13–14, 20, 86–87, 90–92
Proceso, El, (The Process), 32
professionals
   exile of, 8, 92
   repression of, 16
   surplus of, 50, 52
   wages of, 30, 32–33
professors, wages of, 53
pro-Fidelistos, 38
   see also loyalists
promiscuity, 48
prostitution, 11, 30–31, 40, 43, 48, 53, 57
Protestantism, 79
Puerto Rico, 10
punishment, 8, 19
   of dissidents, 13, 16, 86, 88, 90
   of emigrants, 92
   for theft, 26

quality of life, 59

race relations, 33, 39–40
Radio Marti, 91
raft people, 92–94
rallies, 14–15
rationing, 22–23, 33
recreation. *See* leisure; sports
reforms, social, 10, 18, 32, 34
refugees, benefits for, 91

religion, 8, 12, 50, 76–85
   see also individual religions
repression, 15–16, 19, 23–24, 43, 70, 79
   of dissent, 8, 86–92
   of political parties, 9, 13–14, 88
   of religion, 12, 50, 85
   in schools, 46–47, 52–53
   see also media, government control of
research, health-related, 59
researchers, 55
resolver, 24–25, 60, 75
Revolution (1959), 8–11, 32–33, 38, 40, 46
   commemoration of, 69, 74
   loss of faith in, 19–20, 23, 52, 78–79, 92
   loyalty to, 13, 18, 42, 49–50
   opposition to, 13, 15–18, 41, 50, 86–92
rich people. *See* upper class; wealth
Roque, Marta Beatriz, 91
ruling elite. *See* Communist Party, membership in; upper class
rumba, 73
runners, 68–69

salaries. *See* wages
Santeria, 73, 80–82
scare tactics, 19
scientists, 32, 50
Secret Society of Abakua, 81
self-employment, 13, 26–28, 31, 36, 43
service workers, wages of, 53
   see also tourist industry
sewage systems, 59
sexual activity, 48, 57
   see also AIDS; prostitution
Shakespeare, William, 70
shortages, 10–11, 22–25, 36–37, 70, 92

see also specific commodities
slaves, 73, 80–81, 83
smuggling, 94–95
soap operas, 65–66
Socialist state, 12–13, 66, 74
   Cuba as, 18, 21, 26, 31–36, 39, 90, 95
   health-care system in, 54–55, 59, 61–62
   training in doctrine of, 45–48, 50
socialized medicine. *See* health-care system
social structure, 32–43
son (music), 73
Soviet Union
   collapse of, 51, 57, 60, 68, 79, 92
   Cuba subsidized by, 8–10, 21–22, 31
   educational system in, 45
Spain, 32, 76
Special Time, 10–11, 22–31, 51–52, 55, 57–61, 68, 92
spirit, Cuban, 23–26, 33–36, 40-41, 64
spiritual hunger, 77
spiritualism, 81–82
sports, 49, 66–69
spy system, 9, 14–16, 36, 46, 64, 85–88
standard of living, 18, 29
stickball, 67
street parties, 71
stress-related health problems, 58
sugar crop, 10, 22, 78
suicide, 58
surgeons, 56

tango, 73
Tattlin, Isadora, 75
taxes, 26–27
teachers, 8, 15, 52–53
technicians, 55
television, 65–66

theft, 26
13th of March tugboat, 94
totalitarian society, 8–21, 73, 88
tourist industry, 12, 27–31, 34,
47–48, 68, 70
see also prostitution
trade schools, 49
Trading with the Enemy Act,
73
trains, 24
transportation, difficulties of,
24–25, 28, 58, 85
travel, 16, 31, 36
trials, 87
see also judicial system
tuberculosis, 57

underemployment, 50, 52–53
United Nations, 54
United States
embargo by, 8, 10, 60, 68, 73

encouragement of
emigration by, 91–95
hatred of, 13, 17–20, 46, 73,
86, 90
universities, 46–47
acceptance into, 12, 18,
49–50, 76
graduates of, 44, 50, 52–53
upper class, 32–33

vaccinations. *See* immunizations
Valladares, Armando, 20
Varela Project, 88–91
Veliz Martinez, Pedro Luis, 91
Venezuela, 10
violence, 16
Virgin of Charity, 82–85
vitamin deficiencies, 57
volleyball, 66–67
volunteer service, 36
voodoo, 81

wages, 16, 24, 28, 50
government control of, 32,
39, 43
walking, 58
water, shortage of, 24
wealth, 13, 18, 26–27
transfer of, 31, 40, 42
weapons training, 46
weddings, 38–39
West Africa, 73, 80
women, status of, 33, 39–40, 47
work ethic, 47–49
working class, 92
writers, spying on, 15

yambus (dance), 73
Yoruba tribe, 73, 80
youth, 15–16, 21, 44–46, 78–79

Zaire, 10

Picture Credits

Cover Image: © Bob Krist/CORBIS
© AP/Wide World Photos, 30, 48, 58, 77, 90
© Bettmann/CORBIS, 9
© Dominic Bonuccelli/Lonely Planet, 65
© Claudia Daut/Reuters/Landov, 41, 51, 63, 69, 78, 84
© EPA/Landov, 93
© Alejandro Ernesto/EPA/Landov, 67, 72, 74, 82
© Bill Gentile/CORBIS, 49
© Rick Gerharter/Lonely Planet, 55, 61

© Peter Guttman/CORBIS, 27
© Jeremy Horner/CORBIS, 38
© Cindy Karp/Time Life Pictures/Getty Images, 37
© Martin Llado/Lonely Planet, 62
© Amos Nachoum/CORBIS, 45
© Rafael Perez/Reuters/Landov, 14, 17, 25, 35, 89
© Richard Powers/CORBIS, 33
© Jorge Rey/Getty Images, 29
© Tom Smallman/Lonely Planet, 18

About the Author

John M. Dunn is a freelance writer and high school history teacher. He has taught in Georgia, Florida, North Carolina, and Germany. As a writer and journalist, he has published numerous articles and stories in more than twenty periodicals, as well as scripts for audio-visual productions and a children's play. His books *The Russian Revolution*, *The Relocation of the North American Indian*, *The Spread of Islam*, *Advertising*, *The Civil Rights Movement*, *The Enlightenment*, *Life During the Black Death*, *The Vietnam War: A History of U.S. Involvement*, *The Computer Revolution*, and *The French Revolution: The Fall of the Monarchy* are published by Lucent Press. He lives with his wife and two daughters in Ocala, Florida.